# ST. MARK

# The Bible for School and Home

*by J. Paterson Smyth*

*The Book of Genesis*

*Moses and the Exodus*

*Joshua and the Judges*

*The Prophets and Kings*

*When the Christ Came:*
*The Highlands of Galilee*

*When the Christ Came:*
*The Road to Jerusalem*

*St. Matthew*

*St. Mark*

*The Bible for School and Home*

# ST. MARK

by

*J. Paterson Smyth*

YESTERDAY'S CLASSICS

ITHACA, NEW YORK

This edition, first published in 2017 by Yesterday's Classics, an imprint of Yesterday's Classics, LLC, is an unabridged republication of the text originally published by Sampson Low, Marston & Co., Ltd. For the complete listing of the books that are published by Yesterday's Classics, please visit www.yesterdaysclassics. com. Yesterday's Classics is the publishing arm of the Baldwin Online Children's Literature Project which presents the complete text of hundreds of classic books for children at www.mainlesson.com.

ISBN: 978-1-63334-088-6

Yesterday's Classics, LLC
PO Box 339
Ithaca, NY 14851

# CONTENTS

# GENERAL INTRODUCTION

## I

This series of books is intended for two classes of teachers:

1. *For Teachers in Week Day and Sunday Schools.* For these each book is divided into complete lessons. The lesson will demand preparation. Where feasible there should be diligent use of commentaries and of any books indicated in the notes. *As a general rule* I think the teacher should not bring the book at all to his class if he is capable of doing without it. He should make copious notes of the subject. The lesson should be thoroughly studied and digested beforehand, with all the additional aids at his disposal, and it should come forth at the class warm and fresh from his own heart and brain. But I would lay down no rigid rule about the use of the Lesson Book. To some it may be a burden to keep the details of a long lesson in the memory; and, provided the subject has been very carefully studied, the Lesson Book, with its salient points carefully marked in coloured pencil, may be a considerable help. Let each do what seems best in his particular case, only taking care to satisfy his conscience that it is not done through

laziness, and that he can really do best for his class by the plan which he adopts.

2. *For Parents* who would use it in teaching their children at home. They need only small portions, brief little lessons of about ten minutes each night. For these each chapter is divided into short sections. I should advise that on the first night only the Scripture indicated should be read, with some passing remarks and questions to give a grip of the story. That is enough. Then night after night go on with the teaching, taking as much or as little as one sees fit.

I have not written out the teaching in full as a series of readings which could be read over to the child without effort or thought. With this book in hand a very little preparation and adaptation will enable one to make the lesson more interesting and more personal and to hold the child's attention by questioning. Try to get his interest. Try to make him talk. Make the lesson conversational. Don't preach.

# II

## HINTS FOR TEACHING

An ancient Roman orator once laid down for his pupils the three-fold aim of a teacher:

1. *Placere* (to interest).

2. *Docere* (to teach).

3. *Movere* (to move).

1. To interest the audience (in order to teach them).

2. To teach them (in order to move them).

3. To move them to action.

On these three words of his I hang a few suggestions on the teaching of this set of Lessons.

## *1. Placere (to interest)*

I want especially to insist on attention to this rule. Some teachers seem to think that to interest the pupils is a minor matter. It is not a minor matter and the pupils will very soon let you know it. Believe me, it is no waste of time to spend hours during the week in planning to excite their interest to the utmost. Most of the complaints of inattention would cease at once if the teacher would give more study to rousing their interest. After all, there is little use in knowing the facts of your subject, and being anxious about the souls of the pupils, if all the time that you are teaching, these pupils are yawning and taking no interest in what you say. I know some have more aptitude for teaching than others. Yet, after considerable experience of teachers whose lesson was a weariness to the flesh, and of teachers who never lost attention for a moment, I am convinced, on the whole, that the power to interest largely depends on the previous preparation.

Therefore do not content yourself with merely studying the teaching of this series. Read widely and freely. Read not only commentaries, but books that will give local interest and colour—books that will throw valuable sidelights on your sketch.

But more than reading is necessary. You know the meaning of the expression, *"Put yourself in his place."* Practise that in every Bible story, using your imagination, living in the scene, experiencing, as far as you can, every feeling of the actors. To some this is no effort at all. They feel their cheeks flushing and their eyes growing moist as they project themselves involuntarily into the scene before them. But though it be easier to some than to others, it is in some degree possible to all, and the interest of the lesson largely depends on it. I have done my best in these books to help the teacher in this respect. But no man can help another much. Success will depend entirely on the effort to "put yourself in his place."

In reading the Bible chapter corresponding to each lesson, I suggest that the teacher should read part of the chapter, rather than let the pupils tire themselves by "reading round." My experience is that this "reading round" is a fruitful source of listlessness. When his verse is read, the pupil can let his mind wander till his turn comes again, and so he loses all interest. I have tried, with success, varying the monotony. I would let them read the first round of verses in order; then I would make them read out of the regular order, as I called their names; and sometimes, if the lesson were long, I would again and again interrupt by reading a group of verses myself, making remarks as I went on. To lose their interest is fatal.

I have indicated also in the lessons that you should not unnecessarily give information yourself. Try to question it *into* them. If you tell them facts which they have just read, they grow weary. If you ask a question, and then answer it yourself when they miss it, you cannot keep their attention. Send your questions around in every sort of order, or want of order. Try to puzzle them—try to surprise them. Vary the form of the question, if not answered, and always feel it to be a defeat if you ultimately fail in getting the answer you want.

### 2. *Docere (to teach)*

You interest the pupil in order that you may *teach*. Therefore teach definitely the Lesson that is set you. Do not be content with interesting him. Do not be content either with drawing spiritual teaching. Teach the facts before you. Be sure that God has inspired the narration of them for some good purpose.

When you are dealing with Old Testament characters, do not try to shirk or to condone evil in them. They were not faultless saints. They were men like ourselves, whom God was helping and bearing with, as He helps and bears with us, and the interest of the story largely depends on the pupil realizing this.

In the Old Testament books of this series you will find very full chapters written on the Creation, the Fall, the Flood, the election of Jacob, the Sun standing still, the slaughter of Canaanites, and other such subjects. In connection with these I want to say something that especially concerns teachers. Your pupils, now or later, can hardly avoid coming in contact with the flippant scepticism so common nowadays, which makes jests at the story of the sun standing still, and talks of the folly of believing that all humanity was condemned because Eve ate an apple thousands of years ago. This flippant tone is "in the air." They will meet with it in their companions, in the novels of the day, in popular magazine articles on their tables at home. You have, many of you, met with it yourselves; you know how disturbing it is; and you probably know, too, that much of its influence on people arises from the narrow and unwise teaching of the Bible in their youth. Now you have no right to ignore this in your teaching of the Bible. You need not talk of Bible difficulties and their answers. You need not refer to them at all. But teach the truth that will take the sting out of these difficulties when presented in after-life.

To do this requires trouble and thought. We have learned much in the last fifty years that has thrown new light for us on the meaning of some parts of the Bible; which has, at any rate, made doubtful some of our old interpretations of it. We must not ignore this. There are certain traditional theories which some of us still insist on teaching as God's infallible truth, whereas they are really only human opinions about it, which may possibly be mistaken. As long as they are taught as human opinions, even if we are wrong, the mistake will do no harm. But if things are taught as God's infallible truth, to be believed on peril of doubting God's Word, it may do grave mischief, if in after-life the pupil find them seriously disputed, or perhaps false. A shallow, unthinking man, finding part of his teaching false, which has been associated in his mind with the most solemn sanctions of religion, is in danger of letting the whole go. Thus many of our young people drift into hazy doubt about the Bible. Then we get troubled about their beliefs, and give them books of Christian evidences to win them back by explaining that what was taught them in childhood was not *quite* correct, and needs now to be modified by a broader and slightly different view. But we go on as before with the younger generation, and expose them in their turn to the same difficulties.

Does it not strike you that, instead of this continual planning to win men back from unbelief, it might be worth while to try the other method of not exposing them to unbelief? Give them the more careful and intelligent teaching at first, and so prepare them to meet the difficulties by-and-by.

I have no wish to advocate any so-called "advanced" teaching. Much of such teaching I gravely object to. But there are truths of which there is no question amongst thoughtful people, which somehow are very seldom taught to the young, though ignorance about them in after-life leads to grave doubt and misunderstanding. Take, for example, the gradual, progressive nature of God's teaching in Scripture, which makes the Old Testament teaching as a whole lower than that of the New. This is certainly no doubtful question, and the knowledge of it is necessary for an intelligent study of

Scripture. I have dealt with it where necessary in some of the books of this series.

I think, too, our teaching on what may seem to us doubtful questions should be more fearless and candid. If there are two different views each held by able and devout men, do not teach your own as the infallibly true one, and ignore or condemn the other. For example, do not insist that the order of creation must be accurately given in the first chapter of Genesis. You may think so; but many great scholars, with as deep a reverence for the Bible as you have, think that inspired writers were circumscribed by the science of their time. Do not be too positive that the story of the Fall *must be* an exactly literal narrative of facts. If you believe that it is I suppose you must tell your pupil so. But do not be afraid to tell him also that there are good and holy and scholarly men who think of it as a great old-world allegory, like the parable of the Prodigal Son, to teach in easy popular form profound lessons about sin. Endeavor in your Bible teaching "to be thoroughly truthful: to assert nothing as certain which is not certain, nothing as probable which is not probable, and nothing as more probable than it is." Let the pupil see that there are some things that we cannot be quite sure about, and let him gather insensibly from your teaching the conviction that truth, above all things, is to be loved and sought, and that religion has never anything to fear from discovering the truth. If we could but get this healthy, manly, common-sense attitude adopted now in teaching the Bible to young people, we should, with

God's blessing, have in the new generation a stronger and more intelligent faith.

### 3. *Movere (to move)*

All your teaching is useless unless it have this object: to move the heart, to rouse the affections toward the love of God, and the will toward the effort after the blessed life. You interest in order to teach. You teach in order to move. *That* is the supreme object. Here the teacher must be left largely to his own resources. One suggestion I offer: don't preach. At any rate, don't preach much lest you lose grip of your pupils. You have their attention all right while their minds are occupied by a carefully prepared lesson; but wait till you close your Bible, and, assuming a long face, begin, "And now, boys," etc. and straightway they know what is coming, and you have lost them in a moment.

Do not change your tone at the application of your lesson. Try to keep the teaching still conversational. Try still in this more spiritual part of your teaching to question into them what you want them to learn. Appeal to the judgment and to the conscience. I can scarce give a better example than that of our Lord in teaching the parable of the Good Samaritan. He first interested His pupil by putting His lesson in an attractive form, and then He did not append to it a long, tedious moral. He simply asked the man before Him, "Which of these three *thinkest thou?*"—i.e., "What do you think about it?" The interest was still kept up. The man, pleased at the appeal to his judgment, replied promptly, "He that showed mercy on him;" and on the instant came the quick rejoinder, "Go, and do thou likewise." Thus the lesson ends. Try to work on that model.

Now, while forbidding preaching to your pupils, may I be permitted a little preaching myself? This series of lessons is intended for Sunday schools as well as week-day schools. It is of Sunday-school teachers I am thinking in what I am now about to say. I cannot escape the solemn feeling of the responsibility of every teacher for the children in his care. Some of these children have little or no religious influence exerted on them for the whole week except in this one hour with you. Do not make light of this work. Do not get to think, with good-natured optimism, that all the nice, pleasant children in your class are pretty sure to be Christ's soldiers and servants by-and-by. Alas! for the crowds of these nice, pleasant children, who, in later life, wander away from Christ into the ranks of evil. Do not take this danger lightly. Be anxious; be prayerful; be terribly in earnest, that the one hour in the week given you to use be wisely and faithfully used.

But, on the other hand, be very hopeful too, because of the love of God. He will not judge you hardly. Remember that He will bless very feeble work, if it be your best. Remember that He cares infinitely more for the children's welfare than you do, and, therefore, by His grace, much of the teaching about which you are despondent may bring forth good fruit in the days to come. Do you know the lines about "The Noisy Seven"?—

"I wonder if he remembers—
    Our sainted teacher in heaven—
The class in the old grey schoolhouse,
    Known as the 'Noisy Seven'?

"I wonder if he remembers
    How restless we used to be.
Or thinks we forget the lesson
    Of Christ and Gethsemane?

"I wish I could tell the story
    As he used to tell it then;
I'm sure that, with Heaven's blessing,
    It would reach the hearts of men.

"I often wish I could tell him,
    Though we caused him so much pain
By our thoughtless, boyish frolic,
    His lessons were not in vain.

"I'd like to tell him how Willie,
    The merriest of us all,
From the field of Balaclava
    Went home at the Master's call.

"I'd like to tell him how Ronald,
    So brimming with mirth and fun,
Now tells the heathen of India
    The tale of the Crucified One.

"I'd like to tell him how Robert,
    And Jamie, and George, and 'Ray,'
Are honoured in the Church of God—
    The foremost men of their day.

"I'd like, yes, I'd like to tell him
       What his lesson did for me;
And how I am trying to follow
       The Christ of Gethsemane.

"Perhaps he knows it already,
       For Willie has told him, maybe,
That we are all coming, coming
       Through Christ of Gethsemane.

"How many besides I know not
       Will gather at last in heaven,
The fruit of that faithful sowing,
       But the sheaves are already seven."

# LETTER TO THE TEACHER

Very little preface is here required. Read over carefully Lesson II. on "THE KINGDOM OF GOD" before you begin your teaching. Try to work out for yourself the thoughts just sketched there in bare outline. All through the Gospel of St. Mark keep before you this thought of the "Kingdom of God" as the ideal ever present to the mind of our Blessed Lord—a colony of Heaven to be founded on earth, like the colonies of Rome founded throughout the ancient world—a colony whose laws should be the laws of Heaven; whose work and amusements should be according to the will of "The King;" whose subjects should be those who "suffer long, and are kind, who envy not, who vaunt not, who seek not their own;" and whose future should be in the perfect "Kingdom of God" above. Think of the Roman colony at Philippi, whose citizens so identified themselves with the far-off imperial city, rejecting customs not lawful for us to receive or to observe, being Romans." (Acts xvi. 21). Think of St. Paul's teaching about the colony of Heaven to these same Philippians, so proud of being citizens of Imperial Rome. "Our citizenship is in Heaven." (Philippians iii. 20). Try to press on the children this thought of the Kingdom of God on earth as a colony of Heaven. There are "customs not lawful for us to receive or observe, being members of the Kingdom of God." Try to teach them the real, practical religion implied in being members of that Kingdom. Teach them that Bible-reading, and Prayer, and Sacraments are not in themselves religion—the work of the Kingdom—but rather the *indispensable* source of strengthening and stimulating power for performing that religion, that work of "The Kingdom." Show that the Incarnation, the Atonement, the coming of the Holy Ghost were all necessary parts of this ideal of Christ.

The story of the founding of the Church in the early chapters of the Acts is included as part of this book. We cannot say that the Church is the perfect embodiment of Christ's ideal; but it is the best approach to it that humanity has attained. Like a sculptor trying to embody a very noble conception in very rough, intractable material, so is the Lord trying to embody His ideal in imperfect humanity. It is very rough, very imperfect; but it is in some degree embodying the conception, and growing more desirous of embodying it, we trust, as the ages go on. Try to make the children feel sympathy with this longing of their Master, to recognise all that they owe to Him, and to see their duty towards that Kingdom of His into which they came at Baptism. Let them think of Him as looking lovingly down upon their individual lives, watching eagerly to help them towards beautiful deeds, rejoicing in their every struggle toward the right, and thinking wistfully of the day when His desire shall be accomplished; when, in the blessed streets of the Kingdom above, "He shall see of the travail of His soul, and shall be satisfied."

Thus may you help to teach your children real religion; not the religion of mere fruitless church-going; not the religion of mere emotions and excitements, which we hear so much of to-day, but the sound, manly, common-sense religion taught them in the *Church Catechism*, "to do my duty in that state of life unto which it hath pleased God to call me."

## LESSON I

# INTRODUCTORY

### St. Mark I. 1-13.

### "The Beginning of the Gospel of Jesus Christ"

(1) It is important to divide this Gospel clearly into Introduction, i. *vv.* 1-13; Part I, Christ's public ministry in Galilee, ch. i.-x.; Part II, His ministry and death in Judæa, ch. x.-xvi. Mark those divisions in the children's Bibles.

(2) In teaching the importance of the Church in God's plan for the world, avoid all arrogant talk about our separated brethren. Try to impress the idea of a divinely guided Society of baptized people, who should all be one—that separations are weakening it and injuring it, and displeasing Christ. Our Church has been to blame as well as Dissenters. Our duty to ask Christ to help us to bring all together again, so that the sin of separation may cease, and the Church of God be strong and united, as He desires.

(3) The game of word-picturing here suggested, if not overdone, is very interesting to children. If the teacher has any vividness of imagination, he can hold

16

them spell-bound, and can impart warmth and life and colour to the Bible story, that will make it most interesting to them.

## § 1. *How were the Gospels written?*

Meaning of "Gospel"? How many Gospels? One. How many separate accounts of it? Are all exactly the same? Why not? Illustrate four separate boys telling of an accident. Would they say exactly same things? Each tells from own point of view what struck him most. One notices something that another does not, etc. So different. But their stories in the main are the same. Show gain of four accounts of our Lord's life and work. Like four pictures of Him from different points of view.

*Which came first, the Church or the Bible?* Which first, the *telling* or the *writing* of the Gospel story? Which would come first to-day in China? Of course, the Church comes first. The Lord first founded a Divine Society, and then through that Society gave the Divine Book. Men come first and tell the story of Christianity, and teach and baptize converts. Then after some years they begin to prepare written or printed Bible. Thus in China to-day. Thus also in early days. Gospels did not begin by Evangelist sitting down one day to compose his Gospel straight off, as we write books. The Gospels are just the stories told in their preaching by the apostles and disciples everywhere, and gathered together and written down after several years had passed. Every day St. Peter, St. Matthew, St. John, and other teachers sent by the Church were telling the stories of Christ's life. St. Matthew told it to Jews in Judæa; St. John to Gentiles at Ephesus. So told in different ways. Each told what he knew best, and what was most suited for his hearers. By constantly telling same things they got to tell them well—to leave out what was unimportant—to dwell on what was most powerful for touching men's hearts. Thus the guidance of the Holy Spirit was preparing for the writing of the Gospels.

The Gospel, therefore, was first *oral*, or spoken. Then people began to write down the separate stories, lest they should he forgotten. Probably many accounts. (See Luke i. 1-3.) But the greatest and best and most perfect were those four which we now have—the Gospels of St. Matthew, St. Mark, St. Luke, and St. John, written by the inspiration of the Holy Ghost, and *chosen by the Church,* under His guidance, to be preserved and taught, while the other accounts gradually vanished away. Remember it was through the Church that God gave and preserved the Bible. Remember, then, that the Church of Christ is a very sacred thing, and very important to be kept in mind. It is God's appointed means of helping the world. It is the Divine Society founded by Christ. It existed many years before a word of the New Testament was written. It prepared the Gospels under the guidance of the Holy Ghost. It bore witness to them. It preserved them through all the ages. It taught them to the world. It was the instrument used by the Holy Ghost for helping men everywhere to the knowledge of Christ. As far as we can see, there would be no Bible if there were no Church. People nowadays forget the sacred position of the Church. They think it means separate individuals, not one Divine Society. They split it up into hundreds of different bodies, who will not worship together; and then they ask, Where is the Church? Some people don't believe in the Church or its mission at all. (*See Lesson on Acts II.*) They do not understand what grand purposes the Church has accomplished, and what grand purposes God has still for it. Be you careful to remember it. Do all you can firmly, lovingly, prayerfully, to heal its unhappy divisions, for its Master's sake.

### § 2. Who was St. Mark?

Would like to know something of writer of this Gospel. Look at Acts xii. 12. We hear of Mary, the mother of Mark, who had a house in Jerusalem. She seems to have been a person of some means and influence, whose house was a meeting-place for the early Christians in those dangerous days. Probably the Lord Jesus used to go there. Perhaps Lord's Supper instituted in its upper room. Most probably it was the upper room where the Pentecost miracle took place. So the boy brought up in a Christian home. Knew the chief men of the Church. We read that Paul and Barnabas quarrelled about this young Mark (Acts xv. 36-40). Yet he was with Paul afterwards at Rome (Colossians iv. 10; Philemon 24). But Peter seems his especial friend and spiritual father. Came straight to his house to tell of escape (Acts xii. 12). And long years afterwards mentions Mark affectionately as being with him (1 Peter v. 13): "Marcus, my son." Early

Church writers soon after Apostles say that Mark was the "interpreter" of St. Peter—that he put down what Peter taught him of the life of the Lord. So that we might almost call this the Gospel of St. Peter. Pleasant to think of the aged Apostle talking so warmly to his young comrade about all the pleasant memories of the Lord, whom he so enthusiastically loved, and the young Marcus who, as a boy, had probably seen Jesus, and heard the people talk of Him in his mother's house, writing down what Peter told him. Here is the account of a very early Christian named Papias, who is said to have been a hearer of St. John:—"Mark, having become Peter's interpreter, wrote accurately all that Peter mentioned. He did not, however, record in order either the things said or done by Christ, for he neither heard the Lord nor followed Him, but subsequently followed Peter, who used to frame his teaching in accordance with the needs (of his hearers), but not as though making a methodic narrative of the Lord's discourses. So Mark made no error in writing down some things as Peter narrated them."

### § 3. "The Beginning of the Gospel of Jesus Christ"

To-day we have the introduction (ch. i. to *v.* 14). Then comes Part I. (chs. i. to x.)—an account of our Lord's ministry in Galilee; and Part II.—His last visit to Jerusalem, with His death and resurrection. Repeat these divisions. Mark in Bible. Remember them. St. Mark seems a very eager, hurrying writer. He makes his stories, like pictures, very bright and clear, and interesting, and always every picture with Jesus in the midst. But he crowds them in so fast that we can hardly keep up with him. Like a magic lantern, where the pictures are run in very rapidly one after another. In chap. i. he has run in ten separate little pictures, each a perfect and beautiful little story in itself. (See Revised Version, where they are marked by separate paragraphs.) We have only time to look at the first three to-day, and see THE LORD PREPARING FOR HIS WORK (*vv.* 1-14). This portion is the "Introduction to the Gospel." Now shut your eyes, and let me throw the pictures upon the screen.

(a) First is thrown upon the screen—the picture of a wilderness land, with its gloomy rocks and trees, and a rapid river running between the green, reedy banks. There is a crowd of all sorts of people—soldiers, and publicans, and Scribes, and Pharisees—some with anxious looks, some with mocking sneer; and, above them all, a pale, earnest face, and thin, worn form, with a hairy robe and a leathern girdle about his loins. His eyes are flashing sternly; his speech is eager and passionate; he looks like an ancient prophet of God; he makes them think of "Elias, who was to come." And the gay courtiers of Herod, and the rough soldiers of the Empire, and the sneering Pharisees, and the proud Sadducees have to listen to his terrible threats and warnings against sin. He tells all who are sorry for their sins to come down into the river to be baptized, that God may forgive them, and help them to be good. But he says: "I am only a poor humble preacher; I am but preparing for the Great Coming One whom the prophets told you of. He will baptize you with the Holy Ghost." So ends the first picture.

(b) Now shut your eyes again for the next. Here picture after the same manner the baptism of Jesus; prepare your description carefully beforehand. Watch to see if the interest is kept up; if not, let the game of picturing stop. Otherwise, go rapidly on to the third picture.

(c) A dreary desert plain, with the wild beasts swarming about it, looking for their prey, yet passing peacefully and lovingly about the feet of their Lord. Make your picture at the close of the forty days of awful struggle, and temptation, and hunger, when He is pale and wearied with the strain; when the devil has departed, and the angels are ministering to Him. Take trouble to bring out the feeling of awe for the infinite purity and majesty of the Lord. John, before whom the greatest quailed, yet felt himself unworthy to loose the thong of His shoe, so wonderfully was he touched by that majesty of goodness—the fierce, wild beasts forgot their fierceness in His loving presence—the great, strong angels of God, who with a touch could destroy Jericho, were bowing at His feet, rejoicing to do Him service, and wondering that He should stoop to this poor life. What means it all? That the King of the strong angels—the Creator of all things—had come down to poor, humble, sinful men and women, to be their brother on earth, to save their souls, to help them to be good. "God so loved the world." (John iii. i6). Thus our Blessed Saviour prepared for His ministry. Next day we shall see Him fully engaged in it.

## LESSON II

# THE KINGDOM OF GOD

### *St. Mark I. 13-29.*

### "The Kingdom of God is at hand."

The object of the teacher in this Lesson should be to leave a clear, definite impression as to the meaning of "the Kingdom of God." It is most important to get true views about this—to get rid of the selfish thought that Christ lived and died only that I, and certain who believe as I do, should go to Heaven when we die. Teach them of Christ's beautiful ideal—try to rouse their enthusiasm for it—to send them out with an impression of what Christ intended the Church to be. Probably the Lesson here is too long. But with deep, prayerful study of the subject, the teacher who is in earnest can leave the desired impression with fewer words. It might be well to question the children briefly on St. Mark's seven pictures in the Lesson.

### § 1. *The Kingdom of God*

I want to start with a question which will need all

your thinking to answer. What was the favourite, the constant, subject of our Lord's preaching? Almost all teachers who are capable of excitement and enthusiasm about their work, have some special pet subject—Temperance or Missions, or Housing of Poor, etc. about which they get most enthusiastic, always wanting to talk about it, always wanting to rouse us about it; every conversation, every sermon of theirs will somehow lead up to it. People say—Well, that man has Temperance, Missions, etc. on the brain. He can't talk of anything else!

We may reverently say our Lord, too, had one pet subject, one pet enthusiasm, the centre of all His teaching. Every sermon, every parable, referred to it. His whole life has the picture, the model, the revelation of it. It was the vision that filled up all His hopes, all His outlook into the future. What was it? Think. Try again: His very first sermon in this chapter was about it? (*v.* 15). What was it? Yes. THE KINGDOM OF GOD. In Concordance you find it nearly 100 times mentioned: *e.g.*, Mark i. 15; Luke iv. 43; viii., ix. 1 etc., etc.

Again, see parables—Kingdom of God like leaven—hid treasure—seed sown in a field, etc., etc. Main thought in them is the Kingdom of God. (Take trouble to learn and to impress on class that the Divine Reformer, like all the greatest of human reformers, was pre-eminently possessed with one great idea, and that idea was the Kingdom of God.)

### § 2. *What did he mean by it?*

You say He meant Heaven—a happy land to go to when we die? No, He did not. Most certainly He did not. At least, going to Heaven was only a part—the far-off part—of His plan. Whatever He meant, it was clearly something that first of all concerned this earth, that had to begin, and grow, and spread for a blessing on earth. Remember parables about it. What was it like? Little mustard seed growing to a great tree—little bit of leaven spreading through a lot of flour—a little corn of wheat springing up, first the blade, then the ear, etc. Would that mean Heaven? No. It was a little something that He was planting in the world that should spread and grow till it grew to be a great thing—till it leavened all around it. Can you not yet guess what He meant?

Well, let me try to picture what I think was the vision rising in His mind when He thought with glad hope and enthusiasm about the success of His plan. I can imagine that I see it before me. Try and make the picture in your minds as I go on. He sees before Him a sweet, fair vision—a band of boys and girls, and men and women, of true, noble, generous, Christ-like hearts; the sort of people that you can't help loving and admiring; the sort of people that make life so happy and lovely for all around them. Do you know any person like that? It is a small band at first—small, like a grain of mustard seed—only about twenty or thirty, but growing, growing, as the ages go on, till it overspreads the face of the earth. He sees in the vision how everything bad and miserable vanishes before them—all greediness, and lying, and bullying, and spite, and drunkenness, and impurity—all selfishness and cruelty—all poverty, and misery, and pain. They are such brave, generous boys, such tender, unselfish girls—such noble, self-sacrificing men and women, in some degree like the Lord Himself. They care for nothing but what is good and true. They fear nothing but grieving their Lord. Their chief thought is the service of the Kingdom—making all life around them happy, and holy, and beautiful. Would not it be lovely to see a great growing hand like that, increasing every day? Would not they make this a happy, holy, beautiful world? Would not they watch over the sick? help the drunkard? and comfort the sorrowful? Do you think the mean, sneaking sort of boys would dare to be mean and sneaking? Would not the spiteful and untruthful, and selfish girls be utterly ashamed of themselves? Would not many people want to join the ranks of this Kingdom of God, if they saw it so grand, so beautiful, spreading over the earth? Well, that is, I think, the vision of our Lord. That is what He meant by the Kingdom of God. Which should begin where? On earth. And go on whither? To Heaven.

### § 3. How should people enter the kingdom? (v. 15)

Repent: believe in the good news. Which comes first? Would it do to merely tell a lot of careless people that the way to enter this Kingdom was to believe in God's goodness and forgiveness? No. First repent— be sorry. *Then* believe in the love and forgiveness of Christ. Then come forward and be baptized (like soldier receiving the shilling), and thus join the ranks of the Kingdom of God.

## § 4. Recruits for the Kingdom

You remember what was said last day about St. Mark's set of pictures in first chapter. How many? Seven in to-day's Lesson. First is Jesus preaching the Kingdom of God. Six still remain. The first of them (*vv.* 16-21) tells of His going out to enlist recruits for the Kingdom of God (like recruiting sergeant looking for soldiers). Picture—Lake side. Show map. Two fishing-boats. One near. Two rough sailors casting a net into the sea. Names? Could you tell what sort of men they were, whether they were fit for the Kingdom? Could not see their hearts. How did the Lord know? He could see their hearts. Perhaps men with many faults, but sorry for them. At any rate, He knew, and He called them. They knew Him already, and had been attracted by His goodness (if time, refer to John i. 40). What post in the little band of the Kingdom should they have? Fishers of men; what did He mean? Yes. As they caught fish out of the deep, so they should catch sinful, sorrowing men out of the wicked world, and draw them into the Kingdom—into the Church—into the hand of noble hearts who should follow Christ. What a grand office, to help men to be good and happy and love Christ. That work given to us all, not only to clergy. On a little farther. Another boat. How many fishers? How many called? Whom? Perhaps He called Zebedee afterwards, or perhaps Zebedee loved Him already. At any rate, he was probably too old to be an officer in the band, to go fishing everywhere for men like his sons. So you see the Kingdom of God beginning with five or six men; small like a grain of mustard seed.

## § 5. *The Work of the Kingdom*

What is the work of the Kingdom? Doing beautiful deeds. Helping and blessing and comforting people everywhere. See the beautiful deeds beginning. St. Mark's sixth, seventh, eighth, and tenth pictures; what are they about? Casting out devil (*vv.* 21-28). Peter's wife's mother (*vv.* 29-32). Healing the crowd of sick (*vv.* 32-35). Cleansing the leper (*vv.* 40-45). Question briefly, and picture the scenes very rapidly. How sad all this misery and sickness of the world must have made our Lord. What a delightful work was His to cure the evils and comfort the sufferers. Should you like to be engaged in it? Cannot do all the work that He could. Can you do anything of the work of the Kingdom? Comfort people; help them to be good; make life bright and happy for them. Pray for them that they may love Christ and be members of His Kingdom of God. Has the Kingdom grown much now? Yes, a great band, the great Church of God. Are all the members earnest about it? No. That is what spoils it and disappoints our Lord. That is what brings shame upon His Church. The Kingdom of God is the Church. But all its members are not in earnest now, as they were then. Can't you fancy how disappointed the Lord is as He looks upon the careless boys and girls and men and women, who don't care at all to do the blessed work of His Kingdom. What a pain to His heart. He has let you in through Baptism. He wants you to have all the gladness and blessing of working in His Kingdom, and making Him pleased, and making His poor children on earth happy and good. You are members of the Kingdom of God. Story—Frederick the Great examining school on the three great Kingdoms of Nature—Animal, Vegetable, and Mineral. "Now, what Kingdom does this belong to?" (holding up watch). "The Mineral Kingdom." "And this flower?" "The Vegetable Kingdom." "And now, what Kingdom do I belong to?" he asked. Expected answer, "The Animal Kingdom." But the children were puzzled. At last a little girl timidly held up her hand. "Well, my little maid?" "The Kingdom of God, your Majesty." And, amid solemn silence, the great King bowed his head. "Pray God that I may be worthy," said he.

### § 6. *The Strength for the Kingdom*

How can you be worthy? How can you escape disappointing our Lord? Get the strength for the Kingdom's work. See the Lord's example, *v.* 35. You never can do His work faithfully without that. Try hard not to neglect it; not to get up late and run down to breakfast without prayer. Pray to the Lord, whom so many are disappointing. "Lord! I want not to disappoint Thee. I want to be a faithful member of the Kingdom of God."

# FRIENDS AND FOES

### *St. Mark III.*

**"He came unto His own,
and His own received Him not.**

**"But as many as received Him, to them
gave he power to become the sons of God."**

As there is not time to teach the whole chapter, it seems best to omit *vv.* 21-31, as being rather difficult for young children. In senior classes it may be briefly touched. Show their obstinate determination to find evil in Christ, such as already appears in Section I and the bearing of this on His warning shout the unpardonable sin. Show that in Revised Version the correct reading is given, *"guilty of an eternal sin,"* v. 2), i.e., that the sin is rather *indomitable* than *unpardonable*, that the man yielding to such sin, deliberately and persistently rebelling against promptings of Holy Ghost within him, is in danger of getting it so confirmed in him that it will never cease, and, therefore, can never be forgiven. Ask, "Could any penitent be rejected for it?" No, because no *penitent* could be guilty of it. His penitence would show that he was not sinning against the Holy Ghost.

It may be advisable not to read whole chapter at once, but section by section as indicated.

Be very careful to bring out the bright, happy view of God's purpose in giving Sunday.

What was last Lesson about? Kingdom of God. Remind children of Christ's ideal for His Church. Picture to them a band of white-robed Knights of God passing through the midst of this "naughty world" and making all life beautiful and holy as they pass. That is meaning of the Kingdom of God. Chapter to-day divides naturally into sections.—(1) The Sabbath, *vv.* 1-7. (2) Teaching and healing, *vv.* 7-11. (3) The Twelve Apostles, *vv.* 13- 20. (4) The Sin against the Holy Ghost, *vv.* 20-31. (5) Christ's Spiritual Brethren, *vv.* 30-36.

Read Section I. This tells of the Pharisees' anger at our Lord's notions about the Sabbath. Notice that last section of previous chapter is on same subject, and show (Matthew xii. 8, 9) that both occurred same day; that Lord was walking to church at the time through the cornfields. So they followed him into church. What for? To pray to be made loving, and kind, and good? See *v.* 2. What wicked, spiteful men! Did not like Christ, He was so real and true; hated sham, and cant, and hypocrisy, and sternly rebuked them; they always watched to find fault with Him. Was it right to be careful about keeping Sabbath? Yes; but they were so silly about it, and so spiteful. They forgot God's loving purpose for it. What did they blame disciples for in field? Rubbing corn in hand. How silly! They would make Sabbath a torment. Did God give Sabbath to be a torment to people? What does Lord answer? ii. 27. Made for man, *i.e.,* for man's blessing and happiness. Does God like to see happy faces on Sunday? Like to see us out in fresh air enjoying this beautiful world? Yes, we are His children, and He made Sunday for our happiness, and recreation, and rest. No Latin, or sums, or hard school-lessons to-day for boys and girls. No work for tired men and women. What an awful world if no Sundays! God says to us every Saturday night, "Come ye apart and rest awhile. I want you to rest and be happy." "This is the day that the Lord hath made: let us rejoice and be glad in it." Is it not good of our Father in Heaven? What a shame to make it gloomy.

But we have another part of us besides bodies? Souls. And God, who wants us to be happy, knows that a good, noble, beautiful life will best make us so. He says, "If my children only think of rest and amusement, they may forget about goodness and about my love for them, and so lose their highest happiness. The busy men and women may forget Me in the hurry of their work, so I want to remind them about Me every Sunday, and keep them near to Me." Emphasize the two sides. (1) The rest and recreation for the body. (2) Helps and reminders for the soul. And all *for the purpose of our good,* to make us happy, and holy, and loving to God and man.

Now the Pharisees forgot the happy meaning of Sabbath. Thought of as of a taskmaster's order to his slaves.— "Don't do this, don't do that on Sabbath, or else I will punish you." Our Lord was vexed at the way they were spoiling God's beautiful gift, and so He often, in order to teach them, intentionally broke through their silly rules—intentionally worked miracles on Sabbath—broke the Sabbath, they would say. This angered them greatly. Now return to story of this disturbance in synagogue. How began? What ailed man? One of the old, lost Gospels says he was a stone-mason, and had told the Lord that he could not earn bread for his family. Picture—village church—man on seat—arm hanging dead—his eager eyes fixed on Jesus. Jesus' pitying eyes on him. Suddenly He speaks out—what? Now see the Pharisees whispering and watching. Oh, this wicked Sabbath-breaker! going to heal a man on Sabbath! Hear them call out to stop Him. "Is it lawful to heal," etc. (Matthew xii. 10). His reply (Mark lii. 4). Is it best on Sabbath to do *good*, as I am doing, or *harm*, as you wicked, spiteful people are doing? What did they say? (*v.* 4). How did He feel about it? (*v.* 5). Angry. Is not anger wrong? No it is right to be very angry with sin, with spite, and bigotry, and hypocrisy. It was right to be angry with teachers who were turning people against the loving Father, and spoiling His blessed Sabbath gift. Our Lord often angry with such. But was it vicious anger against the men, that would make Him like to hurt them? See next word "Grieved at," etc. That is the right anger, to love God so greatly as to be angry with all sin, yet grieved and sorrowful for the sake of the sinner. All this time the poor man waiting with his dead arm by his side. What next? Could he stretch it forth? Was it not dead? Yes; but when Christ told him, the poor fellow tried to do it, and *with the effort to obey came the power.* So with us—weak, powerless—can't love God; can't conquer sin, can't be truly faithful. But let us say, "Lord, I can't love you much; I can't serve you as I should; I can't be good as I ought; but, Lord, I'll try!" and *with the effort to obey will come the power.*

Do you think the poor stone-mason was glad? And the people? And the Lord? Were the Pharisees? What do? Went out to make plans against Him, and so went on and on in this wicked spitefulness till they brought the Lord at last to the Cross on Calvary.

If not time, next section (*vv.* 7-13) may be dismissed with a few questions, so as to give more time for following section (*vv.* 13-20). Read section. What about? Calling the twelve Apostles together. Had He not called them already in forming first ranks of His Kingdom of God? Lesson II.—Yes; but He was then only calling recruits— rank and file. Now wanted chief officers of His Kingdom to guide and rule it after He was gone. Very solemn task. See how He prepared for it (Luke vi. 12, 13). Think of Him going out alone in the late evening, and walking up that lonely mountain. He could not be happy without prayer, and enjoying the presence of His Father. There all the long, dark night He was in His deep prayer—in His great happiness. And then in the early morning the disciples come crowding after Him, and many of the people of the place. So He looked on the little band who had so willingly come to Him, the beginning of His Kingdom of God on earth. He loved them all. But all not fit to guide and rule. So He who knew all hearts picked out the right men. They were the first rulers of His earthly Kingdom—the first bishops of the Church.

They afterwards ordained other men to preach and teach as the Church grew bigger, and placed some as leaders and bishops, to take their own places when they were gone; and so down through all the ages comes the line of the bishops and clergy of the Church, the first of the line being appointed by the Lord.

How many? Name them? What did he purpose for them? (*v.* 14). That they might be *with Him* in his own immediate company. What a blessed position! Beautiful thought. He wants His teachers to be in close company with Himself—the clergy and Sunday School teachers to be much in communion with Him, and then go out to tell others about Him. What their chief work? To preach. In some things they were very different? Some fishers—others not. One collected taxes. One, Simon the Zealot, opposed the taxes. Peter—bold, fiery, impetuous. Thomas—desponding and doubting. Nathanael so simple and guileless. John so deeply affectionate, etc., etc.

But in one thing all were alike. What? All loved the Lord, and wanted to please Him.

LESSON I.—Boys and girls very different in manner and disposition—illustrate from class. Do these differences make you unfit to be Christ's disciples? What is the one thing in which all His disciples are alike? All love the Lord, and want to please Him. What does He call them at the close of this chapter? (*v.* 35).

LESSON II.—He first calls members into the rank and file of His Kingdom—to be His disciples—to love Him, and want to please Him. From them He picks out those for special work. Perhaps He will want some of you by-and-by as missionaries, or to do some other great work for Him at home or abroad. If so, He will call you again. Should you like to be called by Him to do great work in His Kingdom?

# THE MYSTERIES OF THE KINGDOM OF GOD

*St. Mark IV. to v. 25.*

**"If any man willeth to do His will,
he shall know of the teaching."**

Close your eyes, and make this picture in your minds. A great mass of people, in their bright Eastern dress, crowded at the quiet lakeside—a fishing-boat lying at anchor a few yards away—and One sitting in the fishing-boat speaking to the crowd. He and they together are watching with interest a scene upon the hillside behind. And yet it is a very ordinary scene. Bring it into your picture. A large field upon the hill-slopes, with the rich, brown earth freshly turned up by the plough—a pathway running across it to the farmer's house—the grey rocks here and there peeping up through the earth—the bunches of thorn pulled up in the near corner, leaving many of their roots in the soil behind them; and above it all, the chattering and fluttering of wild birds over the head of a sower, as he scatters far and wide his golden corn seed.

Together they watch this scene, and then suddenly from the boat the Lord calls to them: Hearken! listen! Immediately they are all attention, wondering what He will say or do. "See that sower sowing his seed? See where the seed is falling, and what happens to it?" Again they turn to look at the sower in the field. Now what do they see? Where do they see the seed falling? How many different sorts of soil? Name them. Yes. 1st, on the pathway going up to the farmer's house, trampled hard through many years of trampling. 2nd, on *stony* ground? No; little stones in ground would not destroy growth—but *rocky, i.e.,* where the grey rock, rising through the earth, shows how shallow the soil is there. 3rd, on thorny, where thorns had been grubbed up, leaving some of roots behind. 4th, on the good ground.

Now keep your eye still on the field. What became of seed on pathway? On rocky ground? On thorny? On good ground? Notice the first did not grow at all. The second grew for a while, and then died. The third kept on struggling in a half-withered, useless state. The fourth grew well, and bore good fruit.

Now we may turn away from the field and the seed. The Lord wanted to teach by means of these of another field and another seed. This sort of teaching is called? Parable? What is a parable? Yes. Or it is a something in the outside natural world that is very like something in the inside spiritual world: Why are they so like? Because both worlds are of God, and He works much in the same way in both.

Some of Christ's hearers did not care about the spiritual world, and did not want to know anything of it. But some had earnest hearts, and were anxious to learn. How? (*v.* 10). "To you," He said who come with simple heart and honest desire to know, I will teach the secrets of the Kingdom of God." So He begins:

(1) The seed is? (*v.*14), the Word—the Word of God. What sowing of it had just been going on? Yes; He thought of Himself like the sower in the field, scattering the good seed over that crowd of people—they were the field. Did the corn seed succeed equally well all over the field? Does the seed of the Word? What is wrong when it does not succeed? Is it the seed? No; the soil. Seed is all good. Both the wheat seed and the Word seed. God has given both a miraculous power—to live, to grow, to bear fruit. But the seed is tender, delicate, can be lost and spoiled by neglect, bad soil, etc.

Does anybody else act as sower? Clergy, teachers, friends, who speak to each other about holy things. Look round Sunday School now. See all the sowers in all the classes scattering the seed. Think of preacher in pulpit to-day, scattering seed through the church. Is it not solemn to think of the picture which our Lord gave of the hearts on whom it is sown? How many sorts? Like what sorts of ground?

(a) Now take the first. When the Great Sower sows, by the Bible, or the preacher, or teacher, some falls on the pathway. Think of this class—this school—and say solemnly to yourself: "Some falls on the pathway." Meaning? Yes. That some—let us hope they will be very few—will let it fall unheeded off the hard, trampled surface—"in at one ear, out at the other." Children in school, men and women in church, who will listen without a single sin brought to remembrance—without one resolve for a better life; without one wish breathed up to God for strength to do that duty brought before them in the message to-day. What an awful *waste*. Think of the poor heathen wanting it, and not getting it, and we so shamefully wasting it. But that is not the worst. The hard hearts will get harder by it, like the pathway on which the sower often walks. Next Sunday the surface will be a little harder on account of the neglected seed and sowing to-day. And who is watching to snatch it away (*v.* 15). Did you ever feel him do it? Well, watch out next time. When some whisper of God comes in sermon or lesson, or in friend's advice, or in conscience rousing you to resist meanness, or lying, or ill-temper—if you refuse to receive it or let it grow, it will not be there to grow at some future time. Then cometh the devil, like the fowls of the air, to snatch it away. Sometimes you don't feel him; sometimes you do. Sometimes the sharp end of the seed seems to stick in soil, to get a chance of growing, and you feel conscience pricking you to do something or resist something; but you refuse. You can almost feel the devil snatching away the good seed that was trying to get hold.

Why does any heart become like pathway? Whose fault? Is it God's? Whose? Yes. When Christ has warned us that heart is in danger of getting harder, the seed of being snatched by the angels of Satan ever watching us, then it is our own fault if we do not watch and pray and be earnest. Suggest to form the habit of silent prayer for preacher and people when sermon begins. If much done, would greatly improve both preaching and hearing.

(b) Next sort of soil? *Rocky*, not *stony;* remember the distinction. How did it grow? Fast, because of warm rock below, warmed by the sun. But then what happened? Now, what sort of people meant? Better or worse than stony? Better, received the word, thought it very lovely to be a Christian, touched to tears by thought of Christ's love. Very gushing, emotional sort of people, greatly moved at Confirmation or such times. But no root—no holding on. The important thing in religion is not warm *feeling*, but earnest *doing*—eager clinging to Christ. In the little acts at home, in the little temptations at school, always trying to be loyal. Some people can't feel very deep emotion about Christ's love; they feel almost cold-hearted. But they say—Never mind. In spite of coldness of heart—in spite of discouragement of trying to do right and failing—I will cry to the Blessed Lord, who is so good and so loving. I'd rather bear anything than be disloyal to Him! Blessed is he that endureth!

(c) Third sort—Thorny ground. Seed sown where thorn roots remain, and both spring up together. These are still better than the last soil. They keep on caring to be good, but only in a half-hearted way. They are uneasy about religion, and give half the heart to God, and half to the cares and anxieties of the world. And so they have just enough religion to worry them; not enough to make them happy. But what are they to do? Must have cares about work and home and support and getting on in the world. Yes, but remember our Lord's advice: "Seek ye first the Kingdom of God and His righteousness, and all these things shall be added unto you." Settle first of all to give your heart to God, and then, as His child, work hard and hopefully at all worldly things. Put God first. Bring all else to Him that He may help and bless you, and then struggle and work will not sadden or harm you.

(d) And last of all we have the good ground. They who hear the word, and accept it, and bear fruit thirty-fold, sixtyfold, and a hundredfold. No time to talk further of this. Take away solemn thoughts about this sowing of God's seed. Pray to the Great Sower that we may not disappoint Him. Pray to Him especially for the teaching in this class and in this school, that in the harvest of life there may be fruit of our sowing:

> "Lord of Harvest, grant that we
> Wholesome grain and pure may be."

# LESSON V

# A STUDY IN CONSCIENCE

### *St. Mark VI. 1-30.*

### "Their conscience bearing witness."

There are three subjects in this section:—The Carpenter, The Mission of the Twelve, The story of Herod. It seems best to choose one for *special* emphasis; so we take the last. It will require a good deal of thought and care and sympathy to teach this Lesson. First get the class in touch with subject. Question out of them their own experience of conscience pleading, approving, condemning. Don't be afraid that subject is too deep for them. They probably know more about it than many of their seniors. Read Lesson in Joshua on Achan.

(1) First section (*vv.* 1-6) is about "The Carpenter." Where was this scene? Synagogue at Nazareth; own country. People assembled in church. A strange preacher to-day. Yet not strange; they recognise Him as He speaks. But so wonderful a sermon never preached there before. Such wisdom; such powerful speaking; such sweet, loving words. What did congregation say about sermon? about preacher? Yes; astonished, but

43

jealous and prejudiced. He was not a gentleman; never been to colleges of Rabbis. They remember Him as a young carpenter, making benches and tables for their houses and yokes for their cattle. True, He was very good and kind and brave and self-sacrificing. He had worked to support the poor widowed mother when Joseph died. But He was only a common carpenter, and it was impertinent of Him to set up to teach His betters. They would not listen. They were offended in Him.

Teach here briefly that "rank is but the guinea stamp." "'Tis only noble to be good." Teach the nobleness of all honest work. Christ teaches us how grand a workman's life can be. He teaches that all work may be religious, even a boy's or girl's learning lessons. He was learning His lessons one day from the doctors and teachers (Luke ii. 46), and He called it "my Father's business." So all children's lessons may be. St. Paul speaks of servants' or slaves' work. It must be done well, he says, "for ye serve the Lord Christ." (Colossians iii. 24).

Question briefly on next section (*vv.* 6-13); but as the Apostles and their work have been referred to in earlier Lesson it may be lightly touched on here.

(2) Now comes a "study in conscience." After getting class to realize conscience in themselves, as already suggested, read from *v.* 14 on. Here is Herod, a Sadducee. Not believing in angel, or spirit, or resurrection—yet terrified at the new Teacher's coming. What does he think? Friends say that it is Elijah, or one of the prophets. "No," cries this terrified unbeliever, "it is John, whom," etc. How could he think that? Ah, it was the

torture of conscience within him. It was God's judgment already begun in his soul. Did you ever feel any pain of conscience? Even if nobody knew or could punish? How awfully solemn. Who put this conscience in us? What does it do? It judges every action; it gives approval or condemnation, makes happy or miserable. It warns of God's punishments hereafter. What an awful thing. Yet what a blessed thing. God's gift to keep us doing right—to frighten us from doing wrong.

Why Herod frightened? (*vv.* 16-20). Herod had committed a great sin. Put away own wife, and took brother's wife to be his. Do you think his conscience told him he ought not? Yes: even in the worst and most ignorant it does that. Some people think that Herod when a boy had good teaching from a religious foster-mother. They read in Acts xiii. 1, of a good, holy man, his foster-brother; and they think, and probably rightly, of a godly home, a good foster mother, two boys growing up side by side—one, to be a tyrant and murderer—the other, to be a teacher of the Gospel of Christ. At any rate, whether he had this help or not, be sure conscience pressed him not to do this sin. But he would not obey, and so he injured and weakened his conscience, and got his own way. Show the evil of resisting conscience. Every time that conscience says, "you ought," and you reply, "I will not," it makes conscience much weaker for next fight with sin. Every time you obey it grows stronger. Was it not good of God to make Herod's conscience hurt him?

Did God give him up now? No. A brave, true man felt it was his duty towards God and towards Herod to speak out boldly. Who? Never mind if he should die for it; he must do the right. And so he did a very brave and dangerous act. What? (*v.* 18). He wanted to save Herod, and make him stop his sin. God was giving Herod's conscience another chance. Did John touch his conscience? Yes (*v.* 20). He feared him. *Kept him safe* (R.V.). from Herodias. Heard him gladly. Did many things of what John advised. Reformed in many ways. See how, in God's mercy, his conscience was striving again with him. It seemed as if God would conquer and Herod repent. Did he? No. He "did many things." Would not do the great thing that God wanted—give up his awful sin. So conscience again defeated, again weakened and wounded. Herod made a worse man. Whose fault was this? God's or Herod's?

Steadily worse and worse grew Herod. Constantly defeating and trampling on conscience, till it lost its power. Now the awful scene in the banquet-hall. What a horrible birth-day! Picture the scene vividly in all its details. Half-drunken king. Shameless dancing girl. White, set face and gory head on the table. That noble, fearless prophet, who had tried to save him. What an awful pass to come to through always resisting conscience, and, therefore, resisting God.

Now nothing remains but agony and remorse. Never more will Herod have a happy birth-day. Look at his terror (*v.* 14). Day or night, working or sleeping, he was never safe from the horrid vision. The dead face, the gory head, horrible, ghastly, threatening. Awful power of conscience to venge itself. Illustrate *Dream of Eugene Aram*, etc. Conscience no longer power to lead him right, only to torture him. Lower and lower he fell. This is first connection with Christ—terrified. Next time, he wanted to kill Him (Luke xxiii. 7-13). Third and last time, with his men of war, he mocked the Lord, and set Him at nought.

Learn the power of conscience. Given through God's love to keep us right. Danger of resisting it. Duty of obeying it, and praying to God to make it see His standard more clearly, and keep us to it more firmly.

If during this week conscience has to strive with you, say, "It is God's love trying to save me and keep me back." Lift up heart to Him to help you.

## LESSON VI

# THE CONSIDERATENESS
# OF CHRIST

### St. Mark VI. 30 to end.

### "An high priest who can sympathize with our infirmities."

The whole lesson is about Christ's considerateness. Do not underestimate the importance of teaching the lesson about holidays here. It is most injurious to children to associate God's will only with work and school, and disagreeable things, and to fancy that He only "puts up with" play and holidays, and laughter, and all that they enjoy. Apply the third section as a "parable of life," as indicated in the Lesson.

### § 1. Considerate for Tired People

Read *vv.* 30-34. Hold up hands, all who don't like holidays. You *do* like them? But does God? Does he not prefer work? You know your school work is God's will for you—sums, and geography, and Latin, and all hard lessons. God's will that you should do them well. But

48

what about the amusements—the games, the fun in the play-ground— the Easter, and summer, and Christmas vacations? What about marbles, and handball, and football, and cycling, and cricket, and tennis? (For girls mention girls' games.) One great use of studying our Lord's life is the finding out his opinion about matters of ordinary life. Now, here we have Him and His disciples going for vacation.

Disciples just returned from their mission; dead tired after tramping from village to village in the hot sun, preaching and arguing with unwilling hearers. What did they tell Him? (*v.* 30). And even while they told Him, had they rest? (*v.* 31). Many coming and going; crowding, clamouring, bustling; "no leisure so much as to eat." And the kind thoughtful, considerate Master knew it had been a hard pull for them, that there had been overstrain of mind and body, and that the best thing for them was perfect change and rest. And don't you think he needed it Himself even more? He had far more work and strain than they, and the news that had just come did not make it easier. What news? (*v.* 29). (See also Matthew xiv. 12.) His cousin John murdered by Herod. He knew it was good for them all to get away from the work and the people—away amid the fields, and woods, and mountains—to walk and talk together; to rest body and mind, and to commune with God. What did He direct? (*v.* 31). Were they not kind and thoughtful words? What do they teach us about our holidays, and rest, and recreations? That they are part of religion, as well as work is; they are God's will—they are God's pleasure for us.

Is it right to teach boys and girls that only lessons, and work, and sickness, and disagreeable things are God's will, and not to tell them that the games, and amusements, and merry romping everywhere are God's will, too, so long as wrong-doing is kept out? Would your parents like to see you never playing, or laughing, or enjoying yourselves? Would God like it? Parents want you to enjoy life. Does God? Yes; far more than parents do. Not lazy, constant idling. He hates that. He delights in hearty work. But He delights, too, in hearty play after work. Therefore, always remember in the midst of games and holidays that God rejoices in His children's enjoyments. He intended the lambs to skip and jump in the fields. He intended you to laugh, and play, and be full of happiness. Only one thing He forbids in your play, because it would spoil your happiness and your lives. What? Sin.

### § 2. Considerate for Hungry People

Read *vv.* 34-44. Saw His considerateness for tired people. Now see it for hungry people. Did He get the holidays that He wanted for Self and disciples? Did He get away from crowd to rest? Why? (*v.* 33). I wonder if you would like, just at holiday times when very tired, to find holidays stopped. So here. Crowds saw them going, and noted direction, and came swarming after them—no rest; no quiet. Did He get vexed? (*v.* 34). His whole thought always for others. Far away in the country, many miles from towns and shops. What did disciples say? Jesus too considerate to do so. Doubtless very tired and faint Himself after that tiring day. So could understand their weariness, and the misery of walking many miles to find a shop. Tell me the conversation (*vv*. 37-39). Astonishment of disciples. What could He do with so little food!

Directions about seating them—in *ranks*—word means "garden beds." Evidently they were placed in regular rows and squares, and, with their bright-coloured dresses, looked like a number of huge flower-beds. Why so arranged? That all should be orderly, and none passed over. Like arrangement at big Sunday School treat. How many "flower-beds" would there be if all fifties? How many if all hundreds? Women and children sat in other rows separate. Therefore, easy to know number (*v*. 44).

Now, see the gaily dressed groups, like garden-plots, a huge crowd, and the five little barley-loaves in Jesus's hands. How the people would stare and wonder. What could He do? First He looked up to Heaven and blessed them. His thoughts were always of Heaven and thankfulness. *(Refer here to grace before and after meals.)* Then? Then? Gave to disciples and they to poor hungry people—men, women, and children. How thankful the mothers would be to see the hungry children fed by Him. How glad He would be, for He so loved children. But how could five loaves feed 5,000? We know not. With God all things are possible. Does He ever do that miracle now? Would you be surprised if I had seen it done last year! How? Farmer put in a bushel of corn in ground, and left it, and God made it into fifty bushels! That miracle is going on every year.

It was nothing difficult to our Lord. It was His ordinary work. He is always doing it. So the "water turned into wine." (John ii.). Nothing strange or difficult in it. It is God's everyday work, only just done then in a shorter time. In vineyards of Italy the vine roots suck up the moisture out of the ground, and God turns it into wine. To us all these things are miracles. To God they are easy, ordinary things.

Notice how considerate he was for these people's wants. He loved men's souls, and helped and saved them. Yet He did not think of people merely as "souls" to be saved, but as men and women to be helped in every way. He is always like that. While thinking of the danger of sinful human souls, He thinks also of the burden of weary human hearts, and the hunger of starving human bodies. He loves to bless us, comfort us, help us, but, above all, to make us noble and good.

## § 3. Considerate for Frightened People

Read *vv.* 45-52. Midnight. He is alone on mountain-top. What doing? Yes; He is always longing to be at prayer in communion with the Father. Praying probably for the world, for the poor people whom He had fed, for disciples. Where were crowds? Where were disciples? How situated? Did He know and see? Did they know that He was looking at and thinking of them? Like the poor troubled, frightened people in the world to-day. Is He looking at and thinking of *them?* Do they know? Some do. Most people doubt or forget that there is One always looking down, caring more than their nearest and dearest for the hard struggle of life. Just as on the mountain-top that night, so always. What did He do? Why? Bring out the thought of His care and consideration in going to help and cheer them, and apply it to the help He gives to frightened strugglers still. "Be of good cheer, it is I; be not afraid." Carry on the story, and apply it as a parable of life. When they received Him into the ship, the storm ceased, and there was a great calm. Show how that happens still when they receive Him into the ship.

# LESSON VII

# DIFFERENT TREATMENT FOR DIFFERENT SOULS

*St. Mark VII. 24; VIII. 21.*

**"He careth for you."**

Remark on the different way in which the Lord treated different people, as shown in this Lesson. Surely we must believe that there was a meaning for it, each soul being treated in the way best fitted to help it. So God has his different ways of treating souls now. Keep before you the object of getting the children into sympathy with His blessed purpose for the world, and desirous to be helpful to Him in it.

## § 1. *The Canaanite Woman*

Read the fuller account in St. Matthew xv. 21-28.

In Joshua and Judges name the accursed people, to be driven out for their wickedness? Canaanites. Here, 1,000 years later comes one of this accursed race to our Lord. But was she very wicked?

Tired and persecuted, the Lord withdrew to the north for rest. He and His disciples could be tired as well as we. "Let us rest for a little; don't tell people." (*v.* 24). No use. The report of the great Teacher and miracle-worker had reached the north. One poor heathen woman had heard of His kindness, and sorely wanted help. Could not be kept back. She knew little of religion; but knew He was kind and powerful. "O Lord, save my little daughter. Cast out the devil." Bitter disappointment. Dead silence. Is He going to refuse? She struggles closer—"Lord, Lord, help me!" No use. He will not answer. Even the disciples plead for her, in order to get rid of her. What does He say? "Not meet to take," etc. Oh! how could He, so kind to others, be so harsh to her? What did He mean? Used the Jews' usual word of reproach for Gentiles—"dogs." Does she get up in a rage? "He called me a dog." Ah, no; she thought of the mad convulsions and horrible sufferings of her child, and she saw, too, something in His face not so cruel as His words. She will humble herself to the dust. She will force Him by her earnestness. And as she thinks of the little dogs under the table, a brilliant thought comes. She will catch Him in His own words: "Not meet to throw it to the dogs." "Yes, Lord, it *is* meet to do it (see R.V.), for even the little dogs eat of the little children's crumbs." What did she mean? Who was the Master? Who the children at His table? Who the dogs? Yes. She thought of the Jews as the children in the Father's house, and she said: "Lord, let me be even as a little dog. I don't want to claim a child's part; but I will not leave the table until you throw me the dog's crumbs. Even if you spurn me or drive me away, I will still follow you, I terribly want your help. I have at any rate a dog's claim."

Wonderful faith. Wonderful love for her little girl. No longer could the Lord restrain Himself. "O woman," etc. (Matthew xv. 28). Had He been unwilling before? Why so hard to her? We can only guess. He treated different souls in different ways. Probably He saw hers was a great soul, worthy of a great testing. He wanted to draw out and strengthen her faith. Must have been something in His look that kept up her faith all the time. Now she gained not only her daughter's cure, but a blessing for her own soul. He did not deal thus with other souls. See deaf and dumb in this Lesson. Each soul treated in a way suited to it. Teach here the power of intercessory prayer, and the lesson of faith, even when prayers not answered at once.

### § 2. The Deaf and Dumb Man

Read *vv.* 31-37. St. Matthew (xv. 30) tells of a great multitude, lame, blind, dumb, maimed. St. Mark just selects one of the cases to tell of more fully—deaf and dumb. Can you do dumb alphabet? Why necessary? They cannot hear. So our Lord here made signs, touched ears and tongue, to show what He was about to do. But first took aside from multitude. Treated people differently, probably according to spiritual state. One healed in crowd—one taken aside—one healed with a word, another with a touch—one healed without even asking—one, as Syrophenician in this Lesson, only granted her desire after a great struggle. Treated each as was best for each. Why lead this man aside? Probably to make a deep impression. Think of the two alone. Lord looking with sympathy into the eyes of the poor mute. Giving him as much attention as if no one else in the world but himself to be healed. So often with people now. Healing from sinful life. Takes them aside by sickness or sorrow, that they may look, as it were, into His face, and be healed. Think how glad and grateful this poor fellow would be when he could enjoy all human speech and all beautiful sounds. How he would remember the Lord, who was so good to him. Nice to see how glad the crowds were. Even His own direction could not keep them still. They would insist on going all round to tell how good He was, and how powerful.

### § 3. *Feeding the Four Thousand*

Read ch. viii. 1-21. What is this section about? What other miracle of feeding? Were they two different miracles? (*vv.* 19, 20). What difference between them? Why did He perform this miracle? (*v.* 2). In case of Syrophenician had He compassion? In case of deaf and dumb? Yet He treated each differently. Show? First—almost refusal. Second—granted when asked. Third—did not wait to be asked. Notice the eager zeal of these people. Three days with Him out in the wilds. Food all used up. He also full of zeal for their good; teaching noble truths; healing the sick. What a heavy, tiring strain, for three days, denying Himself rest, food, sleep. Now had compassion. Was it for Himself, since He was so tired? Never thought of self, but only of others. Think of that compassion looking down on the poor world to-day, with its wants, and sorrows and temptations. Is it just the same now? Yes.

> "There is no place where earth's sorrows are so felt
>     as up in Heaven;
> There is no place where earth's failings have
>     such kindly judgment given.
> For the love of God is broader than the measure
>     of man's mind,
> And the heart of the eternal is most wonderfully kind."

No need of saying much about this miracle, as we have had one like it in last Lesson. But think of the stupid dulness and want of faith even in His own disciples. See their question, *v.* 4, and the conversation in the boat afterwards, *vv.* 15-20. So all through His ministry. They could not sympathize with His noble thoughts about love to others and the glory of self-sacrifice. They could not even believe in His greatness and His power. How lonely for Him. He had come down from Heaven, where all hearts were in sympathy with Him, and all through His earthly life He had to bear that loneliness of spirit. Don't you think it would be a pleasure to Him if His disciples were feeling eager with Him about good; sorry with Him about the sins and sorrows of men; willing with Him to give up all for God and their brethren?

Are Christians now different from these disciples? Are we? Let us think more of this. Think about this beautiful plan of His about the Kingdom of God (Lesson II). Pray that we may be more in sympathy with Him; eager with Him about righteousness; sorry with Him about trouble; willing with Him to give up what is dearest for the sake of God and our brethren.

# THE GLORY OF SELF-SACRIFICE

### *St. Mark VIII. 27; IX. 8.*

**"Whosoever shall lose his life for My sake shall save it."**

In this Lesson it is best to pass over some of the details, and concentrate attention in the one thought— the Glory of Self-Sacrifice—the Ideal for the earthly life, and the actual in the heavenly life. Christ's lessons about self-sacrifice teach the first; the story of the Transfiguration teaches the second.

Two questions of which I want you to find the answers to-day:—(1) What is the glory of the earthly life? (2) What is the glory of the heavenly life?

### § 1. *The Glory of the Earthly Life*

Read *vv.* 27-38. Question closely on *vv.* 27-31. Distinguish questions, "Whom do *men* say?" "Whom say *ye?*" What were the guesses of the multitude which they heard of? What do these guesses show? No ordinary life. All felt that the beauty of that character, the wonder of those miracles, could not be explained in ordinary way. Something wonderful—divine. They could not understand the real explanation, so they guessed as well as they could. Next question? Answer? How did they know? They knew the O. T. prophecies of the Messiah, and nobody could be in Christ's close company without seeing how God-like he was; and besides, they were divinely helped to understand Him (Matthew xvi. 17). They, who of all the world knew and loved Him best, felt sure that He was no ordinary man like themselves, but the Christ of God. *Vv.* 27-34.—Strange teaching followed—what? Why? Perhaps to keep them from thoughts of an earthly kingdom; perhaps to teach them what the Christ-life meant. How did they receive it? (*v.* 32). It surprised and disappointed them greatly. No grandeur; no greatness; no shouting of loyal crowds at His feet. No; but a poor, spoiled life; a poor, despised, insulted man, persecuted and murdered. How could that be for the King of Heaven? God forbid! Hear Peter's astonishment (*v.* 32). Why so puzzled? Could not understand the real glory of life, the glory of self-sacrifice. They thought that success and prosperity and happiness and earthly glory would be the life worthy of the Christ of God. Would it? Did His life show much of seeking for such? What did it show? That He thought self-sacrifice for others' sake the noblest of all things. Even if it led to insult and mockery and death, it was a life grander and worthier of the Son of God than all the glory that the world could give. Which do you think the higher and better—to make yourself happy, or to make others happy? Which does our Lord think?

*Vv.* 34-38.—Therefore He began to teach them what in God's sight is the highest glory of life—what? (*v.* 34). "If any man will come after Me, follow in My footsteps." Some of these disciples wished to, some of you children wish to. How do it? By resolving to make yourself happy, comfortable, rich? No. By taking up the cross. Doing right when it is painful, for Christ's sake. Thinking of others' happiness more than your own. Being willing to lose what you like best for sake of Christ and for sake of others. (Illustrate from children's ordinary lives.) Thus Christ's life taught: "I am going for sake of others to lose self, to lose life, to spoil My life, as the world would think. He that would follow Me must do the same."

Did Christ lose happiness by self-sacrifice?

Shall we really lose happiness by giving it up for others and for God? No. In some wonderful way we get happier still. The inward peace of God and His blessing on our lives make up for all. So our Lord says (*v.* 35). He that is willing to lose everything for the sake of God and right, he shall gain beyond his wildest hopes. Tell me, then, what our Lord thinks the glory of our earthly life?

## § 2. *The Glory of the Heavenly Life*

Now we come to next part—Glory of the Heavenly Life. There, too, love and self-sacrifice are the chief glory. But there is more in the heavenly than in earthly glory.

Read ch. ix. 2-8. Question closely on details. Refer to parallel accounts in Matthew xvii., Luke ix. Wonderful scene. Vision of Heaven. In the darkness of midnight our Lord and three apostles on a lonely mountain. He was praying (Luke ix. 29). They were what? (*v.* 32). Another time they were sleeping while He prayed (Mark xiv. 32-40). While He prayed a wonderful, awful, glorious thing happened—what? Meaning of "transfigured"? Ever see mass of cloud in the evening, dull, plain, and sad-coloured? Then the setting sun shines on it; transfigures it with golden glory; it becomes full of light and splendour; exquisitely lovely. Yet the same cloud. Something like that. His body, even His clothes, glowing with the beautiful light of Heaven—all white, brilliant, dazzling. Like a prince in disguise who had put on his royal clothes for a moment. "He decketh Himself with light as with a garment." What awe and wonder and reverence in the three apostles at seeing the plain poor carpenter's son, their companion, dressed in His real clothes. How differently they would feel towards Him afterwards!

Two other heavenly visitors also in glorious appearance—who? Think of the terror and astonishment of the apostles when they wakened up. Had they only dreamed it? No (Luke ix. 30). They had been a few days ago wondering that pain and death could come to the Christ of God; and He had been teaching them that pain and death might be very glorious things. And now, just listen to the Heavenly Three. What talking about?

(Luke ix. 31). In all the glory and dazzling splendour they talked of the death of shame on Calvary. Did they think it something to be ashamed of? No; it was the glory of the heavenly life, too, this glory of self-sacrifice. Think of the Heavenly Ones who had seen the Lord, and talked about this perhaps before He came down to earth. Think of them and the holy angels watching and thinking and talking about it in Heaven; and now these two talking about it with Him on earth. Think:—

(1) What a delightful world in the great Hereafter, where all is love, and nobleness, and self-sacrifice; where no selfish thought could exist. If it did, it would rise like an ugly little cloud in the clear sky of heaven, and everyone would be troubled by it till it melted away in the light of God's presence. Think of the glory of the heavenly life, where we shall have glorified, transfigured bodies, too; where all eternity will be occupied in planning unselfish delights for those about us, and rejoicing in the presence of the great, unselfish God, whom, at last, we are able to understand and love as we ought.

(2) Think of that same unselfishness as the glory of the earthly life. Only one perfectly unselfish life ever on earth. He lived the heavenly life here. He wore Himself out trying to help, and teach, and comfort men, and then set His face steadfastly towards Calvary, to be despised, and rejected, and tortured to death for the sake of the very people who hated and murdered Him. Then He said to all who would follow Him that they, too, must live the life of self-sacrifice, the life of the "Kingdom of God." Shall we not all try? Care for others' happiness.

Bear painful things, and do unpleasant things for others' sake and Christ's sake. How could we help doing it, even if it were only to give Him the satisfaction of seeing us do it? He shall see of the travail of His soul, and shall be satisfied."

# THE POWER OF FAITH

*St. Mark IX. vv. 14-33.*

**"All things are possible to him that believeth."**

The importance of faith is the main lesson here. With senior classes be careful not to let them confuse faith, which is praiseworthy, with credulity, which is blameworthy. Faith in Christ is not the believing certain facts about Him without sufficient evidence. Faith in Christ means faith in a person—faith in a character—faith in an infinite justice, and power, and love, and nobleness, and generosity. Try to teach this well. In those days of foolish talk about "believing," it is of the deepest importance. It is easy to see how faith thus understood leads to a noble life.

Recapitulate last Lesson. Now mark the contrast. On the mountain, transfiguration—glory—heavenly communing—down on the plain, confusion, and anger, and unbelief, and the agony of a poor boy under the power of the devil. Such is the contrast between heaven and earth.

Picture the scene that met our Lord. A poor boy crying out, and foaming at the mouth; the miserable father blaming the disciples; the disciples worried, vexed, disappointed, with an excited crowd about them, and the Scribes jeering and questioning. "Ah! you have failed. Why don't you cast out the devil? You have not power, Your Master has not power," etc. What a wretched change after the glory of the transfiguration! Like Moses coming down from mount (Exodus xxxii.).

Suddenly they see the Lord. They are amazed. Why? Probably the majesty and dignity of the transfiguration remain. Perhaps the heavenly glory not yet faded away, like Moses (Exodus xxxiv. 29). Running to Him, they salute Him. Evidently people glad to see Him always. Disciples glad to get relieved from difficulty. Like a victorious leader, He turns the tide of victory. He sharply asks Scribes—what? Takes disciples under His protection. Did they answer? Why not? Who did? Tell me his pitiful account of his boy. What does he say of disciples?

Repeat Christ's rebuke. To whom? To all—scribes, people, disciples. How long shall I be with you before you profit by my teaching and presence? (See John xiv. 9.) What does He direct to do with boy? No fear as to *His* success—He is the Lord of all power and might. What happened next? This is a strange fact in our Lord's casting out of devils. The kingdom of Satan is stirred into fierceness by the nearness of Christ. Missionaries tell of similar experiences in India and China to-day— exhibitions of Satanic possession and terrible violence when pleading with souls for Christ. What an awful thing to see the poor boy writhing, wallowing, foaming. Evidently the father can't stand it, as he interrupts his account with an eager cry—what? (*v.* 22). *"If thou canst!"* Why did he doubt? Because of disciples' failure. Anything like this now-a-days? Doubt and dishonour of Christ because of disciples' failure? People say—We don't believe much in Christianity—it does not seem to have much power in lives of religious people. Sunday scholars, and Church-goers, and communicants do not seem to differ much from others in ill-temper—peevishness—selfishness, etc. What a shame to bring dishonour thus on Christ's power! Why do they not differ from others? Because not read faiths and effort, and prayer. Because not in deep earnest to win the power and strength from Christ. Try to remember that all your failures are counted against Christ by careless people and so they bring dishonour on Him.

What does Lord say to this doubt? (*v.* 23). What a wonderful fact—that Christ so wanted to be trusted. His power seems hindered by doubt and distrust. To be trusted is such a help to Him. (Note meaning of "faith" in Introductory Note.) See the Syrophenician woman, and His delight in her faith (Matthew xiii. 58). Could do no mighty works because of unbelief. So He wanted this man to trust Him. Could he? Was it wicked of him? No! he could not help it—so discouraged by disciples' failure. A man has not it always in his power to believe or disbelieve. In such case should he be blamed? Does God blame him? What, then, does God want? The *will* to trust Him. The *will only* is in our own power. Had this man the will? Yes (*v.* 24). It was a poor weak, little faith. But he wanted it made stronger. People sometimes have doubts now about religion. Is doubt always sinful? Certainly not; often they can't help it. When are doubt and unbelief sinful? When they are wilful. When they come from carelessness or an evil life. Many a poor doubter has had to cry out eagerly like this man: "Lord, I believe; I want to believe, help my unbelief!" And this is real faith, and God accepts it and strengthens it. If one says, "I can't believe in God," the answer should be: "Have you prayed in deep earnest—as for dear life—for light and faith?" If not, the doubt is your own fault.

See how Christ accepts the poor man's weak faith. See how he utters His masterly command. What? (*v.* 25). Was He obeyed? Devil departs, leaving him. How? (*v.* 26). Like an outgoing tenant not caring what mischief he does." (*Fuller*). No power in Heaven, or earth, or hell can resist Christ; and we have permission to come and ask Him to use His Almighty power. Surely we could get far more blessing of every kind if we only came to Him oftener and more earnestly. That is the secret of all power for good.

Has Satan power over people now? Over men and women? boys and girls? How shown? Ever see poor drunkard falling into the fire and into the water? Who is making him do that? Ever see boy or girl in fierce rage, or using evil words, or doing dishonest deed? It is Satan makes him do it. He has not troubled to resist Satan, and so Satan got strong. Who can save him? Parents, and teachers, and clergy can advise him, but can't cast out Satan. Who can? (*v.* 28). "Bring him unto Me." No case too hard for Christ. He has all power in Heaven and earth. He can make every one of us live such brave, noble, pure, beautiful lives, that it will be a very delight to live. Let us keep earnestly desiring it, and earnestly asking it, and it will be certainly done. "This kind can come out by nothing save by prayer." (*v.* 29, R.V.)

# LESSON X

# CHRIST AND THE CHILDREN

### *St. Mark IX. 33, to X. 17.*

### "He called unto Him a little child."

Teacher study parallel passages in St. Matthew. Recapitulate lesson of Transfiguration. After Transfiguration they went on through Galilee (*v.* 30), and came to Capernaum. On the road the Lord overheard a dispute going on behind Him. They thought He had not heard. He knows all our thoughts and words. Utterly confused and ashamed when, as they sat in the house, He quietly turned to ask them—what? Felt like school-boys caught in some wrong that they thought was not known. Already had learned enough to be ashamed of dispute. What was it about? Why this dispute now? Perhaps because Peter, James, and John chosen to be at Transfiguration. Perhaps the high praise given to Peter at Cæsarea Philippi. Lord was sorry to see this bad spirit. Tried to teach them the law of greatness of the Kingdom of Heaven—what? (*v.* 35). Meaning? THE HIGHEST GREATNESS IN GOD'S SIGHT IS THAT OF

71

HUMBLING AND FORGETTING SELF FOR THE SERVICE OF OTHERS. THE LOWEST POSITION IN GOD'S SIGHT IS HIS WHO IS ONLY STRIVING AND STRUGGLING FOR HIS OWN GAIN AND GREATNESS. All class repeat this. Take case of boy or girl at home. Describe to me the sort that will be highest or lowest in God's sight? Take case of merchant, politician, etc. By such questioning into details make the subject real and practical to the children.

Such was Christ's sermon. What was His text? Strange text. Imagine preacher to-day in church saying before sermon, "This is my text," and lifting a child like M___ on to the pulpit. Called unto Him a little child; perhaps one of Peter's little boys, as this was probably Peter's house. Did the child come? Yes. Don't you think the children in that house would be fond of the Lord who often came in amongst them? Do you think children soon find out who is fond of them? Some people don't care for children. Some greatly love them—which sort our Lord? Did He tell the little chap to stand away from Him while He taught this lesson? What then? Lifted him on His knee; put His arms around him. I don't think He could help doing that whenever He got a little child near Him (see ch. x. 16). He was so fond of them, they could not help being fond of Him. You could not either if you saw Him and knew Him, as you will one day in Heaven. He was greatly popular with children. They ran to Him, clung to Him in His arms, shouted "Hosanna" to Him. What a joyous friend for children. Full of sympathy for their innocent pleasure and mirth. Children, cling to Him; don't disappoint Him.

Think of these eager, grasping apostles, each

worrying and striving to be greater than the others. See them looking at this innocent little child taken from his play, and wondering in his little heart how he came to be taken such notice of. No thought in his mind about their wretched strivings and ambitions. Quietly nestling in the arms of Jesus; living in the present, not fretting about the future, he is just the example to teach them Christ's lesson: "Unless ye become like this child." How? Does it mean that child sinless? Or any child? Tradition—this child was afterwards the great martyr, St. Ignatius, thrown to wild beasts in Rome. Perhaps true. Probably fond enough of our Lord to die for Him. But surely not sinless. All mankind fallen. Even little children need a Saviour. But the Lord wanted to teach childlike spirit. Children, unless badly brought up, are innocent, contented, kindly—not self-conscious, not supercilious, or making class distinctions. Not fretting about the future. Peacefully, quietly trusting their parents, and living just "one day at a time." The hard world hardens and spoils us. The Lord says, "Keep the child-like heart in you. Be as little children in the Great Father's home. Not worrying or fretting for greatness, but loving and trusting the Father, and gladly doing His will."

Watch Him still with child clasped in His arms. "Whoso receiveth," etc. (*v.* 37). How He loved children, and commended them to men's care. But oh! how angry if one led them wrong! What does He threaten? (*v.* 42). Meaning of "offend"? Think of Him looking at little boy and letting His thoughts run on into future, when people should tempt that child away from God.

How awful Christ's anger! Shows how great His love for children. Show me how this anger could be deserved (1) by parent or teacher; (2) by one of you. Worst sin in God's sight is to tempt another to do wrong.

Meaning of verses 43-48. Tell us to cut off hand or foot with knife? What? If tooth very bad—no rest or sleep. What do? Pull it out. Painful? Yes but worse evil to leave it in. Whatever habit, or companionship, or occupation causes you to stumble, away it must be cast, even if as dear as right hand or eye. Tell me some such? Desire for drink; wicked companion, who is pleasant; occupation dangerous to modesty or truthfulness, etc. However painful, cut it off. Better to suffer—better to die— than to sin. So the Lord says, and He should know. How awful sin must appear to Him!

Ch. x. 13-17.—Here He is with the children again. They brought them—for what? (*v.* 13). What good was it? If not old enough to understand His teaching, could they receive any good from His blessing them? Surely yes; else He would not have acted as He did. Disciples rebuked them. Perhaps thought it would do no good to them. Some people think that still, when we bring children to Him in Holy Baptism. Did Jesus say, "Take these children away until they are old enough to understand my preaching"? No. God can do the child good before the age of understanding. So He told Jews to bring infants to Him in circumcision, and we believe He wants us to bring infants in Baptism, that He may bless them. Here again we have anger showing love. How? (*v.* 14). Never in His life before was He so "sore displeased." No such strong expression ever again used of Him. It seems to have been the most offensive and criminal thing to keep children back from Him. Just as He felt before about leading them astray. And again His great heart went out to the little ones, and one by one they were clasped in His strong arms, and blessed with great spiritual blessing. What did He say to disciples? "Suffer," etc. "Of such is the Kingdom of God." Remember what we learned about Kingdom of God in Lesson II. What was it for? To march as young "knights of God" through this "naughty world," blessing and gladdening it, and helping all around us to live beautiful lives for God. Are you too young and foolish to be members of the Kingdom? Is it not a beautiful life to put before you, to live as members of His Kingdom of God on earth, and then march on at death through the golden gates to the higher Kingdom of God in Heaven?

# THE DIGNITY OF SERVICE

### St. Mark X. 17-46.

**"The Son of Man came . . .
to serve, and to give His life."**

Picture scene of last Sunday's Lesson—crowd round our Lord—child in His arms. "Suffer little children," etc. Outside the crowd on the road; a young man walking up and down—restless, eager—waiting to speak his earnest question. What question? Was he satisfied with himself, like the Pharisees? Point out how lovable he was; and yet deep in his heart the feeling that he lacked something. What? Right desires? Earnestness? Humility? Belief in God? No. (Let children prove that he had these.)

Like doctor probing and questioning, Christ treats him to find out for him his lack. First rejects the careless, superficial use of word "good." You call me good. Why? Is it that you believe I am God? God only is entirely good; entirely able to satisfy your desire for good." Now next question? Answer? (*v.* 19). Was it true? Yes. But you might keep from lying, and killing, and stealing, and cheating without real religion. What is real religion? The reaching out of the heart towards God; the willingness to do everything for God's sake and righteousness' sake. Had he that? Yet he had a desire for it, and it touched our Lord deeply. (See *v.* 21.) He looked into his heart, saw his striving for better things—his desire for highest, noblest life. Then with his great love for him, He saw that only one terrible test would show him his lack. It was an awfully hard test for a rich, prosperous young man, the favourite of the world. "Give up all and become a beggar, and follow me!" Like a surgeon risking dangerous operation, the only chance for his patient. Would it have been worth giving up all to follow Christ? What would he have got in exchange? The joy of self-sacrifice—of religion—of the favour and approval of Christ, and therefore of his own conscience. In a few months after hundreds did it: Acts iv. 34-37. He was just on the brink of gaining all this, and being happy for ever. Lord watched him. What would he do? His eternal life depended on it? Alas! he failed. (*v.* 22). But also he learned his lack of real religion. His question was answered. May we not hope that he came back again to Christ!

Then the Lord, with sad heart, and disappointed for this young man, told His disciples of the dangers of riches, and the grandeur of service for His sake and the Gospel's. (Question closely on passage *vv.* 23-31. Explain "needle's eye." Gates of towns had little side-gates called "eye of needle," through which only passengers could pass. Camel might push through if beaten hard, or very hungry, but *could not carry his load through.*) In *v.* 30, tell children the joy of giving up all to go and serve as Christ's messengers to the heathen. It may be that this Lesson may be used to send some out from this old Church in like manner to those children of Ireland, who in the olden days were the greatest missionaries of Europe.

Now (*vv.* 32-35) He exemplifies the dignity of service in Himself. How trivial are riches and applause of men in Christ's view. The glory of life to Him was not riches, or comfort, or applause. No, but service. To serve men and suffer for them. To suffer what? (*vv.* 33-34). Wonderful picture. Group of men on the road to Jerusalem—He, the leader, in front, going straight up to be crucified, with the firm resolve in heart, and the glory of self-sacrifice so appearing in His look, so that they were amazed. Felt how grand He was—how far above them. (Caution—Don't be too high flown or over children's heads in talking of this dignity of service. Illustrate from their own lives. Or rather, get them to illustrate by making them remember the pleasure in their own hearts of little deeds of nobleness and unselfish service of others.)

The Lord disappointed in young ruler. Again disappointed now. After this beautiful teaching about self-sacrifice, see James and John, and their mother. See Matthew xx. 20. They were His relatives, and thought they could come behind the backs of the others and ask favours. What? What was wrong in request? How does it show they had not rightly learned Christ's teaching? What does He say? (*v.* 38). Meaning of this? Did they know that He meant suffering? Yes; He had just told them (*v.* 33). What did they reply? So they were brave fellows, and willing to suffer for Him; but they wanted to be put highest in glory above the others. If they had really Christ's spirit in them, what would the request be? "Lord, grant us to serve, to be of use in Thy Kingdom, even if it be in the lowliest place." Was the Lord vexed? No. He saw the good in them, as well as the evil. He knew that in the days to come they, like Himself, would know the glory of self-sacrifice. So He answered kindly. Did He promise the thrones? What? (*v.* 39). Pain—self-sacrifice—death for sake of Christ and Gospel. These He thought better than thrones. One day they, too, thought it. For the Lord's prophecy was fulfilled—how? James executed (Acts xii. 2). John exiled and martyred.

Still more disappointment? (*v.* 41). Why indignant? Did the Lord notice it? Yes. Think how disappointing to Him, with all His noble, beautiful thoughts, to have as His closest companions men who could not enter into His feelings at all. Here were they again disputing. Same disease of ambition and self-seeking was in them all. See how kindly He bears with them. Think how His words would draw out all that was good in them. "True greatness," He says, "such as I am following, is to be reached by the way of humility and the lowly service of others. I came to earth not to be"—what? Meaning of "to minister"? The ambition of men is to have many servants—the ambition of Christ was? To serve. Motto of the Princes of Wales, "I serve." What a glory it would give their lives if really followed their motto as Christ did. That was the glory He sought; and He goes on to tell the very height of that glory—what? "And to give His life." What a lovely world Heaven must be when that is the object of aim and ambition. To serve others. To give His life for others. Pray: "Lord, help me to understand Thee, to adore Thee, to follow Thee in my own lowly way in the ambition of service."

# PREPARATION FOR DEATH

*St. Mark XIV. to v. 26.*

**"I lay down My life for the sheep."**

Now drawing near the end—the Cross and Passion. This is the Saturday before Palm Sunday, when the dinner party given in Bethany. Chief priests and Scribes, growing more bitter, determined to kill Him. Just because He was too good, and rebuked their wrong-doing. Wanted all along to do it. Now especially, since He had raised Lazarus ( John xi. 45-53). Why not arrest Him? So they said: "Put it off till after Passover." But Judas promised to manage it for them without waiting, and to arrest Him alone when people not there. So God's purpose was brought about unintentionally at right time and "Christ, our Passover, sacrificed for us."

## § 1. Mary

Dinner party at whose house? Supposed that Simon was husband of Martha, or father of the Bethany family.

See St. John xii. 1-8. Perhaps this party was rejoicing about Lazarus's resurrection. Who brought the box of ointment? (John xii. 3). Lovely perfume like otto of roses, very costly. But poor Mary thought nothing too costly for the Lord. Who grumbled? Who began it? (John xii. 4). Why? Were they right? People grumble thus still when money used for missionary work or beautifying church. Would it be right to neglect orphans and poor to do this? No; but the people who thus give generally give to poor also. Not deprive the poor, but deprive themselves to give to God. So God, who loves self-sacrifice, loves such gifts.

Was the Lord pleased? Nice to feel that somebody cared so much for Him when all were against Him. So pleased that He said something about "memorial of her." Ever see memorial pillar, or tomb, or inscription? What for? What was Mary's memorial? Just a deed of love. Was it as good as a pillar or inscription to make her remembered? Yes, to this day, through the whole world it is talked of. Beautiful deeds are the best of all memorials. (Florence Nightingale, Grace Darling, Carey the missionary, etc.)

### § 2. Judas

Awful contrast. Mary and Judas. The one sacrificing herself for Christ, the other—? Why did Judas grumble? John xii. 6. Awful to think that he could be so bad in our Lord's company. Puzzling questions. Why did Christ, who knew his heart, let him in amongst the Apostles? Perhaps because of His love, that "hopeth all things," and hoped he might repent. Why did Christ, knowing his weakness, let him have the bag? Perhaps to give him the opportunity of splendid victory. Great victory can only be won at risk of great loss. Which would be better for Judas's character—to take away the temptation, or to let him conquer it? So, if bag taken away, he would not steal, because he could not. But would he be any better for that? No. So with your temptations to untruth, or temper, or any sin. Temptation good for making character. It is by conquering temptations that men grow holy. Do temptations always do good? Why not? Did the temptation of Judas? What did he plan? Then they could seize Him and kill Him, and Judas would get how much for his treachery? About £4. Beggarly price for such a sin. It is but a beggarly price that we get for any sin. Almost everyone feels that when repentance sets in.

### § 3. The Last Supper

An upper room. The Lord and the Twelve sitting at the Passover, or rather reclining. (Explain the way of reclining round the table.) It is their last night together, and they are saddened and troubled. And He, too, is burdened in heart. Think of the sorrow to Him who knew all things. Knew that these twelve whom He had chosen to be His closest friends would all fail Him— Peter deny—Judas betray—all the rest run away from the danger, and leave Him. How that great love was disappointed then. And *now* also. But He is thinking of their sorrow, not of His own. St. John tells us how He comforted them (St. John xiv. 1). How like Him—never to think of Himself, but only of others.

Suddenly a startling announcement. "One of you shall betray Me." Did they suspect Judas? Or each other? (*v.* 19). Wonderful humility and brotherliness. Each only mistrusted himself. Could it possibly be me? Surely none of us would do it! Judas, too, asks, "Is it I?" He wants to see if the Lord is as unsuspicious as his brethren. And in a low voice, unheard by the others, Jesus answers him (Matthew xxvi. 5). Should not this have startled him into giving up his sin? Still more awful words followed (*v.* 21). Think of the awful fact, which is true of some today also. Be solemn and earnest, and pray that God will save you from it,

Now wine-cup passed round. Bread and bitter herbs eaten. Now a pause. Something very solemn happening? (*vv.* 22-24). He was now putting an end to Jewish Passover. It pointed in type to Him through all the centuries. He was the Lamb who should be slain. And now the type was about to be accomplished and done with. Instead of it, He would make a new and different festival. He took plain bread and plain wine, and blessed them, and by His mighty power decreed that when this was done by His Church in the days to come, it should be a means of receiving spiritual strength, receiving in some wonderful way His own self into our souls. What says Catechism? What is the outward part? Inward? Benefits of which we are partakers thereby? You can't understand all this mystery; but you can understand at least one of the reasons why people should be regular communicants, and why you should when admitted to it after Confirmation. "Do it always," He said, in remembrance of Me." Don't forget Me. Let this be always the reminder to you of My love, and of the lives I want you to live for Me."

Imagine a dying mother saying to her children: "Do this in remembrance of me. Once every year put fresh flowers on my grave." What a shame if neglected! How it would disappoint and sadden her if she could know. But that is a common sin with careless Christians. Think of this when you see the Holy Table arranged for Communion, and let it remind you of that night in upper room, and of the many who, like the disciples, disappoint and sadden the Lord. Say, "Lord, help me not to sadden or disappoint Thee. Lord, when I am old enough to be allowed to Thy Holy Table, I will try regularly to come in remembrance of Thee."

# LESSON XIII

# GETHSEMANE

## St. Mark XIV. 26-50.

### "Behold and see if there be any sorrow like unto My sorrow."

We are now drawing near the end. We are in prologue of an awful mystery—the Great Deliverer needing deliverance—the Comforter of humanity looking for comforts. Be very reverent and solemn. Make the children feel that they are on holy ground. Teacher should spend much time beforehand in meditating and praying about this Lesson, and trying to enter into the solemn spirit of it.

Read *vv.* 26-32. Recapitulate last Lesson. Last Supper over. His good-bye to them. Had told them of parting—tried to comfort them about the future. Just here were spoken those words of comfort (St. John xiv., etc.). "Let not heart be troubled;" "home prepared for you." "I will come again." "I will send the Comforter to you." Is it not beautiful this loving, unselfish heart —not a thought of self even in that dread hour? He knew of wretched morrow—the betrayal and denial, the judgment, the mockery, the spitting on and scourging, the awful agony of the Cross. But no thought for that, only for the lonely little band that He was leaving. He was always like that. He is like that still in Heaven.

Then they sing a hymn, probably the *Hallel*, the usual Passover hymn, comprising Psalms cxiii. to cxviii. Read a few verses of this hymn. Then out in the bright moonlight they go along the Olivet road. The strain on His heart growing more severe—the intense craving for solitude—for prayer—for the Father's presence. He must be alone in His favourite praying-place. Talk on the road. Peter's impulsive reply. Peter always impulsive—like us Irish people (see again *v.* 47)—big, generous, impulsive heart, always rushing at things, not calm and quiet. Very confident. Not safe to be too confident. Safer a few hours before when he distrusted himself, and said, Lord, is it I?" Be afraid of unaided self. Be very confident in God.

Read *vv.* 32-42. Now approaching very solemn sight. Right on to lonely glades of Gethsemane. All left behind but three. Who? When with Him before? Why bring them? His human craving for friendship in great trouble. He is feeling so lonely and troubled—exceeding sorrowful unto death. "Keep near Me, you three. Tarry ye here," etc. As they tarry He hurries past. He must be on His knees. He must flee to the Father's presence for comfort and help. What a blessed thing for anyone to have such love of prayer and of God. What a blessed shelter in trouble.

Now we behold awful sight. Agony of mind so awful that even He could not bear it. He who was so brave and calm to bear everything. Listen to tortured cry: "O my Father! if it be possible remove this cup from Me." Meaning of "cup."(See ch. x. 38, 39.) What was this cup? Was it the fear of death? Was it the denial, betrayal, contempt, and scorn, awful death upon Cross, with mocking crowds around? Surely not. Bad as all these were, He was too brave to fear them. Even some of His humble martyrs have borne death without fear. What was it? We do not know. Cannot understand. Deep mystery of God. We only know that it came in some way from the awful burden of the sins of the world. "The Lord hath laid on Him the iniquity of us all." All we can see is that it was some awful, intolerable agony of soul that came on the pure, holy Saviour from bearing the horrible burden of the world's sin.

Was it easy for Him to bear it? No. He had laid aside His Divine power—had to bear it as a man. You and I find it hard to do painful things for sake of God and duty. Wonderful and comforting to think, He found it hard too. Terribly hard. "If it be possible, let it pass from Me." How awful it must have been! Is it wrong to feel it hard to do one's duty? No. Duty is all the grander when you feel it hard, and yet do it. The Lord had to force His human will to obey the Divine will, just as we have to do. But He determined to do it, however hard. That was the grand thing. Therefore He can understand our struggles to do it. Can sympathize with and pity us, and rejoice with us when we conquer like Himself. If He had kept His power as God to help Him, would it be half so grand or so helpful to us? What does He say about getting His own will? (*v.* 36). No matter how hard to do or bear, let that be always our prayer. When it comes to praying that, the struggle grows quieter. Like as with our Lord, there comes a great calm—the calm of victory—and "there appeared an angel from Heaven strengthening Him." So with us, too.

How many times did He go to see if disciples were keeping watch with Him? Why? His heart yearned for their comfort—and sympathy. And what did He find each time? Yes. They failed Him—miserably, shamefully. Was He very angry? No. Would you be, if some day in horrible misery you found sisters or mother quietly sleeping while you were suffering? "Much they care," you would say angrily. You would not trouble to make allowances or excuses for them. Not so Jesus Christ. See what He says: (*v.* 38) "Ah!" He says, "the spirit is willing enough; it is only the flesh that is weak." He knew it was not that they did not care, but they were so dead tired, perhaps up previous night with Him. Is it not touching to see Him actually apologizing for them, making excuses for them, trying to look for the good in them where others would only see the evil? Is it not comforting to us to think He is like that—like a father with bad son looking for any little trace of good in him, delighted to find it, making every allowance for him—looking for the good motive at bottom of mistaken action—looking for the sorrow and penitence in his heart, when others only see his faults and his sin. Thank God we have such a loving Master.

# GOD TRIED BY MEN—
# MEN TRIED BY GOD

### *St. Mark XIV. 53 to XV. 15.*

Try to be very solemn and sympathetic in teaching the sufferings of the Lord. Pray very earnestly that God will touch the children's hearts deeply by the story.

Recapitulate last Lesson—Gethsemane, Betrayal, Midnight Arrest. Now at midnight the Court of Sanhedrim assembled—summoned together in the night to be ready when the band came in from Olivet with the prisoner.

### § 1. God Tried by Men

Most astonishing sight on earth. The Judge of Mankind at the judgment bar of men! The Saviour of Mankind about to be killed by those whom He came to save! Think what a mockery. His judges are the men who hated Him for rebuking their sin, the men who sent out spies to trap Him, the men who tried to kill Him. Was there likelihood of fair play? Could these men, with their spite and cant and hypocrisy and self-seeking, form any true judgment as to character of the loving, self-sacrificing Christ? No more than a bat could judge the sunshine. They called witnesses—for what? To find out the truth? (*v.* 55). Determined that He must die. Little they thought that thus they were doing what He wanted. He, too, was determined that He should die.

Picture scene—The palace of high priest probably thus—(1) First the *porch*, with pillars and porter's lodge. (2) From this doors opened into the *court* (*v.* 66), a long apartment open in middle to the sky. (3) Beyond this, reached by steps, the *judgment room* where the trial took place. Get class to make mental picture of it, with the judges assembled, and the Lord before them, pale and tired, with strong cords binding His hands, and "beneath in the court" (*court*, not *palace*, *vv.* 54, 66) Peter and the servants warming themselves. It seems when all fled, Peter and John ashamed, and came back (John xviii. 15); but afar off (*v.* 54); door-keeper knew John, and let them in. This is how we get the account of the trial. They saw it. Tell me about the false witnesses (*vv.* 55-60). Did the witnesses succeed? It seemed as if He would get off free. They could not condemn Him. Was high priest pleased to see it? (*v.* 60). Could not sit still—so angry at his failure, and calm, dignified silence of prisoner. "Why don't you answer?" he cries. Could He have explained this story about Temple? But He knew it would be no use. They only wanted an excuse to condemn Him. Did He get fiercely angry? Did He ever in His life get fiercely angry? Yes (Mark x. 14); but it was for others' sake, never for His own. He could be fearfully angry at one who had led a little child astray; but He could be grandly patient and silent when they were cruelly ill-treating Himself. What a beautiful soul was His! He is trying to make us like that. Are *we* trying? At last the high priest gets an answer. Stung beyond endurance at the quiet silence of the Lord, he asks—what? No more silence now. Calmly, solemnly the answer comes: "I am." And what more? How grand, how God-like the answer! What a mean, unjust trial! If He had said "No," they would say "an impostor." He said "Yes," and they cried—what? Then comes the horrible, brutal treatment. We almost shrink from reading it. Fancy those brutal creatures cuffing and boxing Him; spitting in His face; tying bandages across His eyes, to make Him guess who struck Him! And afterwards the mocking soldiers whipping Him till the blood came, and flinging an old red horse-cloth over His bleeding shoulders, in mockery of a king, and crushing down on His forehead a crown of sharp thorns till the blood trickled into His eyes! Oh, how could they! And He was their God! their Saviour! Is it not horrible? Yet, is it not beautiful to see such noble suffering! And is it not very touching for us?

> "I bore all this for thee;
> What canst thou bear for Me?"

## § 2. *Man Tried by God*

But another trial going on in the courtyard. What? Peter being tried. Poor Peter—found it much easier to be religious and confident in the upper room (ch. xiv. 31). We never know till tested. Ashamed of running away, he had come in now, and tried to seem at ease, sitting with servants at fire, but very frightened. Would they find out about Malchus's ear? Suddenly without preparation his testing begins. How? (*v.* 67). Did you ever tell a lie when suddenly asked, and you had not time to decide? So Peter now. A sudden temptation like that is a good test of us. Cultivate habit of bold, transparent truth, always, and then you will never be taken unawares. Then he tried to escape this girl; out into the porch where the groups of people waited. But the girl followed Him and repeated charge. What happened? How did the third suspicion come? Galilean accent—country brogue. Peter now utterly terrified. What a horrible thing (*v.* 71).

So God's testing of Peter was over. Peter had utterly, shamefully failed. Oh, how could he! With the Master who loved him being persecuted to death, and all the world against Him, would it not be better to suffer anything than desert Him? And in a minute he saw this himself. In the cold, grey dawn outside he heard the cock crow, and just then they were hurrying out the Lord, condemned to death. And as He passed out He gave Peter that one look of unutterable pain that nearly broke poor Peter's heart.

Could Christ ever forgive such a sin? Such sorrow as Peter's will always bring forgiveness. St. Clement tells that Peter never forgot this sin—that whenever he heard a cock crow he would get out of his bed and cry again to the Lord in shame and tears. See how sweetly the Lord forgave him. Even on the cross and in the

Hades world He was thinking of poor Peter. Think of the touching message He left with the angels for the women at the tomb: "Go and tell my disciples a*nd Peter* —Peter, who has denied Me—Peter, who is breaking his heart, and thinks I have cast him out for ever—tell him especially." Oh, no wonder Peter so fond of Him. No wonder that burst of eager, passionate devotion: "Lord, Thou knowest all things; Thou knowest that I love Thee!"

If there is time, there is a very interesting study of another "man tried by God," in Pilate's case (ch. xv. 1-15). Wanted to save Christ, but afraid. See all his shifts and subterfuges to save Him. But could not dare much for the right. So his name in Creed for eternal disgrace: "Suffered under Pontius Pilate."

Lessons—

(1) Is it possible for us to deny Christ?

(2) What Christ deserves from us:

> "I did all this for thee;
> What hast thou done for Me?"

# THE CRUCIFIXION

*St. Mark XV. 15-42.*

**"They crucified Him."**

St. Mark's account of the Crucifixion is short and imperfect. Teacher must carefully study the story in the other Gospels as well. Read the connected account in Farrar's *Life of Christ*, or Malleson's *Life of Christ*.

Must be very solemn to-day. Awful story before us. The story of the first Good Friday. Remember what happened the night before. Arrested, carried to Jerusalem bound, tried, mocked, beaten, accused falsely, condemned. What an awful night! What scenes of hatred, malice, insult! What bitter disappointments! Peter cursing and swearing, that he did not know Him; all the rest running away and leaving Him in His peril. So He was left alone all this wretched night, hurried from trial to trial, before Annas and Caiaphas, and Pilate and Herod—mocked and sneered at for His silence, struck in the face when He ventured to reply, listening to the lying and twisting of His innocent words. Then came the scourging before nine o'clock in the morning, when He was handed over all bleeding to the rough soldiers, to be taken out to Calvary. See the brutal horse-play with Him in barrack-room; the mocking and derision, the shouts of coarse laughter when some soldier thought of the joke of making a thorn crown for the King of the Jews, putting a reed in His hand for sceptre, and throwing an old purple rug over His bleeding shoulders, in mockery of His royalty. Then the horrible thing that we shrink from reading. They pulled away the reed, and kept striking Him and spitting on Him. Remember, this the Almighty God, who loved us and them, and that all this was borne for our sake and theirs.

Now (*v.* 20) the wretched procession through the hot streets with the two thieves, the weary Saviour exhausted after the night of horror, struggling to carry cross, and fainting under its weight. Who carried it with Him?

Now at Golgotha. What a sight of agony to the few friends who loved Him. Who? (*v.* 40), and the Virgin Mother and John too (John xix. 26). Now stripped for the cross—the hands which His mother had so often pressed, the feet which Mary had washed with tears, the sacred breast on which John had leaned, all bared for the coming pain. Then He is extended on the cross. Through hands and feet tear the great rough nails; then He is lifted up to be exposed and mocked at in His agony. Tell me of the three classes of mockers (*vv.* 28-32).

Is it not awful to think that men could treat Him

thus? that many to this day are mocking and neglecting Him, giving Him more pain and sorrow? And is it not very touching to think of the sweet tender patience of Christ? It is just here comes in the first of the "voices from the cross," as He looks on the heathen soldiers and the thoughtless, sinful crowd. He prays not for vengeance on their cruelty, nor for deliverance for Himself. What? (Luke xxiii. 34). Think of the generous nobleness of such a heart as that. If that nobleness does not subdue our hearts, nothing else will.

I wonder if mob heard that prayer. I think so, and that God heard it on their behalf. See how they were touched (Luke xxiii. 48). Do you think the robbers heard it, and did God answer it on their behalf? (Luke xxiii. 42). Did the brutal soldiers? One of them reached up a sponge with wine to relieve His thirst, and their centurion and his fellow-soldiers were so impressed with all they saw and heard (Mark xv. 39; Matthew xxvii. 54). Even for the wicked, bigoted priests it was heard (Acts vi. 7). Let us think of Christ's prayer, and be thankful for it, and be touched by that tender love and pity, that exquisite unselfishness, that at such a time could forget Himself to pray for others, even for His enemies.

If there is time, picture here the Penitent Thief, how he was startled and touched by the prayer of Christ. Poor fellow! he was not all bad, and this prayer set vibrating a long silent chord, stiffened and hardened by long contact with evil. Think of the kindly encouragement of Christ! Think how the beauty of the Christ-character did for him what all the Roman remedial prison legislation had failed to do—wakened within him a craving for the good! "To-day shalt thou be with Me in Paradise." Not in the highest Heaven, but in the great waiting place of Paradise within the veil, where the souls of the blessed dead wait for Christ's coming. Where mentioned in the Creed? "He descended into *Hell*," i.*e., Hades.* (See the word "Hell" in Rev. Version.)

Here question also of the broken-hearted Virgin Mother, and His deep, loving solicitude for her. In all His agony He thought about her future (John xix. 26, 27), and sent her away before the dread crisis of His conflict should come, and she should hear the cry of desolation from His tortured soul.

Now (*v.* 33) comes sixth hour. What o'clock? Darkness lasted until? Dense darkness at noonday; Must have frightened them all. Did they think He would come down from cross, as they mockingly asked? Darkness came as a veil to conceal His awful sufferings. Not merely of body. He could easily bear that. Awful torment of soul. We can't understand it. He knew it was coming on. He sent away His mother, to spare her the sight of it. No human being can ever understand the awful three hours' agony in the darkness on Calvary. He had looked forward to it with dread in the Garden of Gethsemane. We can judge of its awfulness by the awful cry at its close. What? (*v.* 34).

We can only dimly guess at the meaning of that cry. We are on holy ground at the most solemn point in the sufferings of our Lord. There seems but one way to understand it. That He was the Divine Sin-bearer, bearing the world's sin. "He was wounded for our transgressions, He was bruised," etc. (Isaiah liii. 5). God "made Him to be sin for us Who knew no sin." The peculiar punishment of sin is the being abandoned by God. In some mysterious way our Lord had to be made to feel that—some sense of utter desolation—something so terrible that even He could hardly endure it. Yet it seemed necessary to the full bearing of our sin. We cannot understand it. But this we can understand, that it was all "for us men and for our salvation."

For us He was scourged and tortured and crucified. For us He endured the three hours' agony and desolation. For our sake that cry of horror rang out in the darkness.

> "Yet once Immanuel's orphaned cry His universe
>         hath shaken.
> It went up single, echoless 'My God, I am forsaken!'
> It went up from His holy lips amid His lost creation,
> That none of us need ever use these worth of desolation."
> —*Mrs. Browning.*

And now cometh the end. For all these hours He has been hanging upon the cross in awful conflict. Now, after that cry of agony, the conflict seems over, and the weary soul of the Redeemer turns to Heaven with that title of child-like love, which, through Him, ever since is permitted to us all. "It is finished," He said. "Father, into Thy hands," etc.; and having said thus, He gave up the ghost.

Think of the loving words from the cross and the

pleading of that love with the world to-day! How shall we escape if we neglect so great a salvation!

"His tender voice pursues each one,
 'My child, what more could thy God have done?
 Thy sin hid the light of Heaven from Me;
 When alone in the darkness I died for thee,
 Thy sin of this day in its shadow lay
 Between my face and God turned away."

"And we stop and turn for a moment's space
 To fling back that love in the Saviour's face,
 To give His heart yet another grief,
        and to glory in the wrong;
 And still Christ keeps on loving us—loving all along."

# THE RESURRECTION

*St. Mark XV. 42-47, and XVI.*

### "The Lord is risen."

Recapitulate last Lesson. Question briefly on xv. 42-47, pointing out in senior classes what a powerful evidence of our Lord's being really dead we have in *vv.* 44, 45. But the chief part of time and attention is needed for ch. xvi. Try to make class realize the utter desolation of that Sabbath, so that they may better feel the revulsion of the Easter joy. For the main Easter teaching of the chapter see special Easter Lesson. The Ascension and the Missionary commission will come best in next Lesson, Acts i.

Picture the little funeral procession on that first Good Friday evening through the garden of Joseph. Name any of the mourners in it? What a terrible dismal thing is returning from a funeral—leaving body of loved one in grave—going into empty house— thinking of all the long, dreary days of loneliness stretching out in front. All that here. But far worse. Not only lost the

101

dearest, truest friend, but lost all the bright hopes of the future. They had thought He was the Divine Messiah—to redeem Israel—to found the Kingdom of God—to dwell with them always in power and glory. What an awful disappointment and shaking of their trust to see Him arrested, and tied like a common prisoner—helpless in the power of His enemies, mocked and scourged, and spitted on, nailed upon a cross between two common robbers; taunted to come down, and not doing so; bleeding and weakening, and at last dying like any ordinary man; the pale, blood-stained corpse put into the tomb. Surely there is an end of all—their love, their hopes, their future are all buried in the tomb. He could not be the Christ of God, after all. He must have been mistaken.

"And when the Sabbath was past." (ch. xvi. 1). Oh! the misery and desolation of that Sabbath! Judas hanged. Peter going wild with remorse; all the rest sunk in hopeless grief; going to church, perhaps; hearing the prayers said by the cruel priests who had murdered their friend; then the men planning sadly to go back to their fishing and tax-gathering, and the women waiting through the night with spices and ointments—for what? Keep body from corruption. How utterly blind to the great joy before them.

Imagine this scene. Early morning—very early; dim, grey twilight just stealing on the darkness; through silent streets of Jerusalem a little group of weeping women hurrying toward the Calvary Gate. Worrying about some difficulty? (*v.* 3). The gate is reached; away they hurry along the horrible Calvary path, across the garden of Joseph, down to the rock-bound tomb, just visible in the darkness. And then—a cry of frightened surprise—the tomb is broken open, the huge stone is lying yards away amid the grass and flowers! What could it mean? To Mary Magdalene, who was in front, came the horrible thought, "Tomb broken open; body carried off by enemies!" (See St. John xx.) And in wild terror and excitement she rushes away to tell the others. The others go on. Perhaps some dim hope rising in them. What do they see in the tomb instead of dead body? (See also Luke xxiv. 4).

They were the attendants of the Lord in Heaven—were about His path on earth. When? (Birth—Temptation—Agony—Resurrection.) Perhaps these same two in the Christmas chorus at Bethlehem. "Young" (*v.* 5). Perpetual youth in Heaven; perpetual beauty and comeliness; perpetual hope and energy, and keen relish of life; perpetual progress towards perfect holiness. What a glorious life, always doing the good purposes of God, and never feeling tired, or old or weak.

What was the announcement to women? (*vv.* 6, 7). How did they receive it? Amazed—afraid. Too frightened and astonished to grasp the glad news at first. But oh! what delight as soon as they realized it. Not only their Lord alive, but all their old trust and hope restored. He *was* the Christ, the Son of God, after all. He had not deceived them or been mistaken. All that He had said about Heaven and immortality was true—grandly, gloriously true. What a glad, delightful change from the misery of yesterday!

More and more confirmation of glad news. As the women hurried away with their joy, Peter and John came running up. Mary Magdalene had told them about the stone rolled away. They see what? (John xx.)

Then, after they had gone, poor Magdalene came back (*v.* 9), and stood outside weeping. Little she knew what was in store for her! See John xx. Through the dim light and the blinding tears she sees a figure, and she mistakes it for gardener: "Where have you laid Him? and I will take Him away." And then—Oh! we never can understand or realize it. A startled gasp, her heart almost standing still, a voice thrilling and tingling through the depths of her being. "Jesus saith unto her, Mary!" And with one quick bound she is prostrate at His feet. "Rabboni, my Master!" Then away back with her glad news. (*v.* 13).

Next appearance? Fully told in Luke xxiv. 13, etc. Walked along the road, and explained to them the Old Testament prophecies about Himself. So the glad news spread, and the certainty grew.

Then he appeared to the eleven (*v.* 4), and upbraided them for unbelief.

Many other appearances. See Special Easter Lesson. But the most touching of all is not anywhere described. Look back to *v.* 7. Why "and Peter"? What had Peter done? So Peter would be afraid to count himself a disciple now—afraid to come near Him again. Therefore He mentions him especially. Was it not wonderful love and thoughtfulness for Peter? But see Luke xxiv. 34; 1 Corinthians xv. 5. Think what a touching meeting that would be. How Peter's heart would be bursting with shame and gratitude and love.

Lessons.—For the Easter lessons of this chapter, see the Special Easter Lesson.

But do not omit to emphasize the appearance to Peter, and that boundless pity and love that was thinking about him, and feeling for him at such a time as that. No wonder that Peter so loved Him! No wonder that burst of eager, passionate devotion: "Lord, Thou knowest all things, thou knowest that I love Thee." So would it be with us if we could fully know and realize, like Peter, that boundless love of Christ.

# LESSON XVII

# THE GREAT FORTY DAYS

### *Acts I.*

### "Speaking of the things pertaining to the Kingdom of God."

It will be necessary for the teacher to again thoroughly enter into the teaching on "The Kingdom of God" in the second of the Lessons on St. Mark. Understand our Lord's beautiful Ideal for that Kingdom. Get class to see that the object of the Church is the realizing that ideal on earth. If Christians forget that object, they forget the purpose for which Christ wants them in His Church.

Last Sunday story of Resurrection. Fitting sequel now. The "Great Forty Days" between Resurrection and Ascension.

*Vv.* 1, 2. What "former treatise"? St. Luke, beginning history of Church here, refers us back to the foundation on which the Church rests—the Gospel. "Former treatise of all that Jesus *began* both to do and teach *until* the day," etc. The present treatise is of all that Jesus *continued* to do and teach *after* that day. Book not really

Acts of *Apostles*—only acts of two Apostles—it is really acts of our Lord by means of His servants after He had ascended. But was He not gone away from them? Matthew xxviii. 20—"with you always." They felt His presence so close to them. See i. 24. "*Thou* hast chosen," ii. 47. "The *Lord* added." See iii. 16, ix. 17. Wonderful how close and real His presence. So now, also, if only we had faith to see and feel it.

## § 1. Between Resurrection and Ascension

How long with them? (*v.* 3). Was it in same natural, familiar intercourse as before? No; very mysterious— appearing and vanishing; not hindered by doors shut, or any obstacle—yet could be seen, known, heard, felt, recognised as the same Jesus—yet mysteriously different. Why? Resurrection body. Appearances just like the angel appearances that are recorded in Scripture. People sometimes ask, "Shall we know one another after death?" They say, "Bible does not tell." Is that so? Our Lord at Transfiguration was in the glorified body, yet Apostles recognised Him. So now after resurrection. There was a change—wonderful—puzzling; but they recognised Him, the same loving Lord, so good to Peter and the Magdalene, and all of them, just as He used to be. So when we meet those gone before, we may be startled at glory and beauty, but shall recognise manner and turn of expression, and shall recognise the real self of him or her whom we loved. "Wherefore, comfort one another with these words."

## § 2. Mysterious Interviews of the Forty Days

Now, in these mysterious interviews of the forty days what was He talking about? (*v.* 3). Turn back to St. Mark, Lesson II. See how all His life on earth that "Kingdom of God" was His central thought—the chief subject of all parables and sermons. Just as every great human teacher and reformer has certain pet projects and ideals—so our Lord also. This was the subject of all His teaching—the object of all His enthusiasm—the vision which filled up His great outlook into the future. (Teacher should carefully go over St. Mark, Lesson II, and call up our Lord's ideal of a Kingdom of God on earth, whose laws should be the laws of Heaven, whose work, and trade, and pleasure should be carried on according to the will of God.)

Is the Church that Kingdom of God? It is at least the poor human attempt at it. Like a sculptor trying to express his beautiful idea in some rough, coarse stone, so our Lord with His beautiful idea planted in humanity.

See how stupid they were about it. What did they ask? (*v.* 6). Thought He only meant a little Kingdom in Israel, with rulers, and soldiers, and weapons. Did He? What did He mean? Wonderful how He could ever risk His "Kingdom of God" with such stupid men. Why could He? Because He was to be with them, and was sending the Holy Ghost to guide them.

### § 3. *Holy Ghost*

What should Holy Ghost give them? (*v.* 8). Power. Power of riches? Power in war? No. What? Power of *holiness*. A rich or grand Church might not do much good; but a holy Church—an inspired Church—a band of men and women full of power from on high—full of enthusiasm for God, for righteousness, for self-sacrifice—they could accomplish anything. Fancy this whole parish of that kind. What a power! What an army of God! "Fair as the moon, clear as the sun, terrible as an army with banners."

### § 4. *Ascension*

Now, after the forty days what wonderful thing happened? (For teaching about Ascension, see the Special Lesson for Ascension Day.)

After this, gathered together, waiting for the promise. Was the Lord present even after Ascension? Is He now? How were they occupied while waiting? (*v.* 14). Praying for what, think you? Were they expecting answer to prayer? Do you always?

Who were chief members? Notice last mention in Scripture of the Blessed Virgin. Was she worshipped or prayed to, or called Queen of Heaven, or Refuge of Sinners, as she is sometimes now? No. Just a simple, humble disciple, like the others, waiting for the gift promised by her Lord and her God. (In Roman Catholic districts emphasise this.)

## § 5. First Official Act

What was their first official act? Why did they venture to elect a new member of the apostolic body? Why did these Apostles afterwards ordain clergy, as our Bishops do to-day? Who told them to make such arrangements in the new Kingdom of God? Surely we must believe the Lord had given them their directions. The Acts of the Apostles is just the carrying out of His directions of the great forty days.

LESSON.—You have been enlisted as members of that Kingdom of God. When? Can you refuse to serve in Christ's army? To help out that lovely ideal of the Kingdom of God, on which His heart was set—a kingdom of purity, love, courage, self-sacrifice? But do you think you *ought* to refuse? Is He present in that kingdom on earth? See how Apostles felt His presence then? (*v.* 24). "*Thou* hast chosen." How they felt His eye and hand about them! Ashamed to be careless and disloyal. So should we now? (Try to bring home to children the nearness of Christ, His longing after His ideal Kingdom of God on earth, the way in which each can help that ideal in common daily life.)

# THE BIRTH OF THE CHURCH

*Acts II.*

**"Ye shall receive power after that
the Holy Ghost is come upon you."**

Teacher should read over the Special Lessons for Whitsuntide, as throwing fuller light upon this Lesson.

Recapitulate last Lesson. "The Great Forty Days." Then came the Ascension—then the return to Jerusalem to upper room—to wait ten days more—for what? (i. 4). What promise? Remember what said in last Lesson about "power" to be given.

### § 1. *The Story of Pentecost*

Picture the group in that room, meeting day after day for earnest prayer and waiting. How solemn life would seem! How real would be Christ and religion! Day after day they meet, waiting, wondering, expecting they scarce know what.

Then, at last, one of the great Church holidays of the Jews. Enormous crowds of Jews from all neighbouring countries crowded into Jerusalem. Whence? (*vv.* 9-11). The 120 disciples make their way through the crowds early. (*v.* 15). Their morning prayer has begun. If every parish like these on Sunday morning—all with one accord in one place—with one accord in eager prayer for the Holy Ghost—in one place, not scattered into different sects and parties—there would be more of Pentecost results. See them waiting, wondering, praying. Suddenly a most startling thing—the house shaking and quivering, as with earthquake, and they *hear*— what? And *see*—what? And *feel*—what? (*v.* 4). This last was the most wonderful of all—the shaking house and stormy sound and tongues of fire, were as nothing to the great wonder of all which they felt in their own souls. Surely this must be the promised gift—this must be the Holy Ghost—God appearing in mysterious power to equip the new Church for its work in the world! And then they discovered another wonderful thing, that astonished everybody who heard. What? (*v.* 4). People came crowding together to enquire about the sound, as of a mighty wind, and as they crowd around, the disciples begin to speak in the various languages of all the strangers. The Jerusalem people don't understand— it seems mere gabble. What do they think? (*v.* 13). But the strangers know better. Utterly astonished. What do they say? (*vv.* 7-11). Yes, it was really the foreign tongues taught by miracle in a moment. Many think it was to enable them to go and preach to all these nations. It seems a sort of prophecy of what the Church should do in the days to come. To-day the Church sends out missionaries to teach many people in their own tongue wherein they were born. The Bible Society sends out Bible in 250 different languages through the world,

What did Peter reply to the mockers? Not filled with wine, but filled with what? (*v.* 4). Not the excitement of drunkenness, but the glorious enthusiasm for God and righteousness. Some cold, worldly people now-a-days don't believe in this wonderful enthusiasm. It is possible still? Yes; there are people now also very enthusiastic for God, willing to do and say and suffer anything if only they can carry out our Lord's blessed design for the Kingdom of God (see last Lesson). But should be far more people and far more power and enthusiasm. What would accomplish this? More of the power of the Holy Ghost. How get it?

### § 2. *The Birth of the Church*

We name this Lesson "Birth of the Church." Why? Christian Church really began on that Pentecost day. Before that day there were materials collected waiting for the influence of the Holy Ghost, like wires laid in their place waiting for the electric energy that was to infuse them with power. Now the power came. Before that day also there were 120 separate individual disciples believing in Christ and loyal to Him. Now they become One Body, they become "The Church." "There is One Body and One Spirit," *i.e.*, the whole band of Christians became the one body indwelt by the One Spirit. Explain: like human body indwelt by human spirit. That is the meaning of calling the Church the "Body of Christ." It is very wrong to split it up into separate little sects. He prayed "that they all may be one (John xvii. 21). And they were (*vv.* 44-47). And so, with insignificant exceptions, for nearly 1,000 years. Then they quarrelled—split up more and more as years went on. Now more than 200 separate bodies in Great Britain. The beautiful thought of One Body, One Spirit, spoiled by these divisions. Like as His earthly body was ill-treated, so is His mystical body the Church. "By schisms rent asunder." But we must not lose hope of reuniting the parts again. God has all power still. Full power of Holy Ghost, in answer to prayer, would teach all divided Christians to love one another, and give up their disputings, and come together again, and thus accomplish their Master's prayer. Like the separate pools on the shore when the tide is out, all belonging to the same sea, all composed of the same water, yet hopelessly separate until the tide sweeps in, and they all become one. So will it be when some day, in answer to earnest prayers, a great outpouring again of the gift of Pentecost, and we all shall be one. And then we may hope that same Pentecost gift will give us more and more of the *power* of holiness and self-sacrifice and enthusiasm for Christ's work.

### § 3. *The First Sermon in the Christian Church*

Think of the influence of preaching in all ages of the Church. Therefore interesting to think of its first sermon, and its results. First the sermon—(1) Plain, ordinary, not clever or eloquent, but close, manly, personal appeal from a man to men as about something of enormous consequence to them. (2) It was all about Jesus Christ—Crucifixion, Resurrection, Ascension, gift of Holy Ghost. (3) Its courageous tone. Think of that poor coward who was frightened by the mocking tongue of a maid-servant a few weeks ago, and these timid disciples who had run away before crucifixion, now bearding priest and Pharisee and mob, proclaiming in that very town where He had been crucified—the Risen, and Glorified, and Ascended Messiah! Where had they got that power? Surely from Holy Ghost. (4) And then look at results. More than all the results of our Saviour's own preaching throughout His ministry. We cannot understand, but the Lord had foretold it. "Greater works than these shall ye do, because I go to the Father." In some way it was necessary for Him to go in order that He should send down this marvellous power—the Holy Ghost. See the result at once. Conviction—Conversion—3,000 men (*vv.* 37, 41) pricked to the heart and crying out, "What shall we do?" More about this in next Lesson.

### § 4. Lesson

Believe in the Holy Ghost—in the *reality* of His power—for Church—for individual (*v.* 3, "sat upon *each*"). His power is ready to our hand to-day. We who want to be good and holy, who want our Church to be a mighty blessing, pray more and more for "the fellowship of the Holy Ghost."

# THE POWER OF JESUS' NAME

*Acts II. 37; III. 26.*

**"A Name which is above every name."**

Recapitulate last Lesson.—Story of Pentecost—Birth of the Church—The First Sermon. To-day we think of the great *power* which our Lord had sent down upon the infant Church. He was still present in its midst, working by means of it. Remember in Lesson on chap. i. we saw this book, not "Acts of Apostles" so much as Acts of *Christ*, invisibly present in His Church.

### § 1. The First Sermon

Recapitulate from last Lesson. (1) Sermon not eloquent or clever, but intensely earnest. (2) All about Christ. (3) Full of courage. Had Peter ever preached before? Often. All sent out preaching through the country by our Lord. Ever a great success like this? Why not? The mysterious promised power not come. God the Holy Ghost not yet indwelling in the Church. Now see that vast crowd. How perceptible is the mysterious *power!* Often. before they had heard these Scriptures— often had heard of and seen the Lord; but somehow everything seems so different to-day—the prophecies so dear—the purpose of God so evident—the Messiahship of Christ, their own awful mistake and sin—all come with overwhelming power. Thoughts of pain are rising in their hearts. "Oh! how could we be so blind! How could we be so wicked! Remember the Lords' promise (John xvi. 8), "Shall convince of sin." Think of the invisible Christ present and rejoicing! Think of the invisible Holy Ghost touching all those hearts. In a moment a great wave of feeling, and a great cry of penitence from 3,000 hearts. What did they cry? (*v.* 37). What a glorious result if we could have it amongst all careless boys and girls, and men and women, in this town! Is it possible? What prevents it?

Now see Peter's answer. Find this repeated in Nicene Creed? Meaning of "repent"? Some foolish people would have answered that ignorant, emotional crowd, "Only believe." Does Peter? Why not? Because it would be putting it in its wrong place. Repentance is the first thing always. See Baptist's teaching—the Lord's—the Apostles'. Everywhere it is a preaching of repentance first and then putting faith in its proper place. (Children find out texts Mark i. 15; Acts xx. 21, etc.)

Something else besides repentance necessary in order that they might receive remission of sins and gift of Holy Ghost? (*v.* 38). Baptism is the Lord's appointed way of admission to the Church. What was the great use of being admitted into the Church? *There* was the remission of sins and the blessed work of Christ's Kingdom of God on earth; there especially was the presence of Christ and the gift of the Holy Spirit's power; there, too, they would have the teaching and the fellowship of Christian men, and the training for their inheritance in Heaven. Your Baptism has admitted you to all these things. (Catechism, Answer ii.) See that you value and use your privileges.

See how these 3,000 used their privileges. Not scatter about as individuals, each to live his own life as he thought best. No. Members of the Kingdom of God, to be used for blessing the world, must not break loose or be disloyal to that Divine Society. Continued steadfastly in Apostles—what? (1) Teaching; (2) Fellowship; (3) The Breaking of Bread; (4) The Prayers. Such is the duty of Christians to-day—(1) Must keep in the Apostolic teaching. What was that? See Matthew xxviii. 20. No new doctrines unauthorized by Scripture. But is that enough? (2) Must keep also in the great fellowship of the Divine Society, not neglecting or ignoring their brethren, but helping and loving them; not splitting up into schisms and parties at their own fancy. What more? (3) Must be regular at Holy Communion—the great channel of spiritual food. (4) And in "The Prayers." Probably they had soon formed a set of Christian prayers. All the Apostles and disciples in their boyhood accustomed to set forms of prayers. We have remains still of the Synagogue prayer-book, and the Temple prayer-book, and very early Christian prayer-book—earlier than some of New Testament. See how all were thus kept together and nourished for accomplishing the great work that the Lord had left to His Church to do—the establishing of the "Kingdom of God."

Did their new religion make than very miserable? (*v.* 46). Some people have only enough religion to make them scrupulous and miserable. These were *filled* with Holy Ghost—*thoroughly* given up to religion. So they did eat their meat in gladness. It is always so. The way to get *full* gladness out of religion is by *full* yielding of one's life to Christ. See the effect of this enthusiastic religion on outsiders (*vv.* 43, 47). With the same fresh eagerness and enthusiasm (*i.e.*, with the same power of the Holy Ghost) the Church to-day would have same effect. And we *could* have it if we were all determined to have it. (Here correct by Revised Version the dangerous misreading of *v.* 47, "those that were being saved.")

### § 2. The First Miracle

Again see the presence and power of the invisible Lord. It is afternoon; what o'clock? Peter and John going to Church to the evening sacrifice. Arrive at the "Beautiful Gate," with its burnished pillars of brass glowing in the sunlight, and its group of ragged beggars looking for alms. One poor fellow they especially noticed. Never had walked or played boys' games—now carried every day and left at the gate to beg. What does he ask for? What receive? Think of his quick start, his wondering, half-doubting effort to stand, and then—oh! the bewildering delight of it!—to feel the new power tingling through every nerve; to feel himself walking and leaping among the people. "Oh! how good God has been to me!" No wonder he should hurry into the temple, walking and leaping and praising God.

Now repeat the words with which Peter healed him. What great difference between this and the Lord's miracles? Christ was the Master, the Lord, doing everything by His own power—"Rise, take up thy bed and walk." (John v. 8). Peter only a servant—"In the name of Jesus Christ walk." Peter begins his speech by pointing out this. Where? (*vv.* 12-16). Yes, and he goes on to tell them what the same Christ could do for them. What? Question on the main points in this sermon. Contrast murderer with Prince of Life in *vv.* 14, 15. Note the kindly attitude in *v.* 17, so like our Lord's disposition to make every possible allowance for men,— "Father, forgive them; they know not," etc. See the quotation, *v.* 22, "a prophet," etc. Compare St. John i. 21; vi. 14; vii. 40— "This is that prophet." Peter says— By His Name hath this man got "perfect soundness in the presence of you all." By His Name, he tells them, you, too, can get—what? (*v.* 26). What of us to-day, what can we get through His Name? Think of Him standing invisible amongst those early Christians, honouring the faithful calling on His Name. Think of Him equally present amongst Christians here, equally ready to hear all that call upon Him.

# LESSON XX

# INVINCIBLE TRUST

## Acts IV. to v. 32.

**"Through faith subdued kingdoms,
wrought righteousness, obtained promises."**

Recapitulate last Lesson. What miracle? Where? Where was Peter's sermon preached? (ch. iii. 11.) What a daring thing to preach in the very temple buildings about the crucified Christ, within hearing of the clergy and officers who had pursued Him to the death! How very fearless the Apostles had grown. Why? (1) Power of Holy Ghost gave courage and enthusiasm for God. (2) The certainty about the Resurrection and the sense of their Master's presence with them, made them care very little for what men could do.

However, it was not likely they could escape. Who came upon them? Why Sadducees? See *v.* 2. Compare Luke xx. 27. This explains the change of persecutors since our Lord's time. He was so stern against cant and formalism, therefore the *Pharisees* were angry. The Apostles made the Resurrection the centre of all their teaching. (See Lesson for Easter Day.) Therefore

*Sadducees* persecuted. Notice through the Acts how the Sadducees are the chief persecutors. It shows how firmly the Apostles insisted on the truth of Resurrection, and that publicly in the very city where Christ was crucified, and within a few months of the time. What a strong proof of the truth of it! So the daring preachers locked up all night in prison; but what of the hearers? (*v.* 4). Worth while preaching that sermon—aye, and being locked up for it, too! The other Apostles would be, perhaps, uneasy for their comrades; but how happy and busy they must have been that night teaching and baptizing the crowd of new Christians. Surely God was showing Himself amongst them!

Next morning a great gathering together of Sadducees in high position; in from the country and the neighbouring towns, assembled for the trial of these presumptuous preachers. Only a few months ago that same court had met—many of these same members— to condemn Jesus of Nazareth to death. Trouble and excitement since, and much talk of His Resurrection. Very vexatious and disturbing. Their own consciences uneasy, perhaps, at the cruel killing of Jesus—disturbed again now—"intend to bring this man's blood upon us." Now determined to stop this annoyance, and this foolish talk about Resurrection.

They began with a question. What? And straight and fearlessly Peter lets them have its answer. What? (*v.* 10). They cannot charge him with presumption. He is but answering their own question. But what a powerful and fearless answer! "By the Name of Jesus Christ." Ye crucified Him; God raised Him from dead.

His Name has cured this man. His Name is the one hope of salvation for you, proud priests and rulers, as well as for us. Neither is there salvation in any other name than in that of this poor, crucified, despised Nazarene.

No wonder that they marvelled. We should have marvelled ourselves if we had seen those "unlearned and ignorant" fishermen, with perfect calm and confidence, teaching the chiefs of the clergy and rulers. Especially if we had seen Peter, who, through fear of a maid-servant, had denied his Lord a few months ago, now challenging the greatest and wisest of his nation in the name of Jesus Christ.

Did he convert them? No—too obstinate and bigoted. We never hear of a Sadducee being converted. Did they disprove the miracle? (*vv.* 14-16). Did they then, with honest, candid mind, inquire about the Christian teaching? Not they! It was a troublesome teaching, disturbing their consciences, and upsetting their own strange, cold notions of religion. They believed in a God; they read the five books of Moses. But believed not in a resurrection, an angel or spirit. A cold, hopeless sort of creed. Might do for prosperous, aristocratic Sadducees, but too cold and hard for the poor struggling world. How did they settle question about the preachers? (*v.* 18). That plan often tried since, using force against the truth. But God is the God of truth, and must hate all such methods. Did the Apostles obey? (*vv.* 19, 20).

Would you have courage to do that for Christ's sake? They risked scourging—imprisonment—death?

Why? Because it seemed worth bearing anything for the love of Christ, and the joy of knowing that their kindly comrade and friend was really Almighty God in disguise. They saw traces of His presence all around them, and you may be sure Peter did not forget the misery of his late cowardice and the wondrous love that forgave him. What cared he now for applause or shame, for life or death, but only that his Lord might approve of him? Have you any such trial for Christ's sake? Have you courage to do right, even if laughed at? Could you rebuke your comrades for mockery of religion? The same Lord is just as much present now, just as glad of the brave disciples, and as disappointed by the cowardly.

Now, "being let go," they went where? To the faithful, true-hearted comrades who loved the Lord. In all the city these were the friends they most cared for—were most in sympathy with—liked best to be with. That is the great test. When "let go" from restraints, where do we naturally turn? Boy "let go" from school. Young people "let go" from restraints of home. Men and women "let go" from work. Good test of life. What sort of companions, books, amusements do they turn to? Good or evil?

Now think of that little company—weak, afflicted, threatened, in danger of life, yet so strong, quiet, calm in *God*. Ah! that is the secret of strength and peace! Peter and John come and tell them of the danger and the threats. Does it frighten them? Not the least! They go to the Great Refuge. Whom? What Scripture do they quote for comfort? Who do they say were chief enemies? (*v.* 27). But whose will were these enemies doing? (*v.* 28). Listen to the prayer about the threatenings (*v.* 29). Do they pray, "Lord, help us to escape"? Not a bit of it! "Lord, give us more boldness to risk more peril, to dare everything for Thee. All is in Thy hands. What matter though heathen rage," etc.? (*v.* 25). "Lord, look on their threatenings. We leave all to Thee. We care not for ourselves what they may do. What matter about us. We are safe with Thee. Only let not Thy work be hindered and spoiled by our cowardice. Give boldness, give signs and wonders in the name of Jesus."

Did an answer come? How soon? How? The very answers they wanted—more of the power of the Holy Ghost—more boldness. That is the best sign of God helping us—to be growing more brave and strong and determined and successful in fighting our temptations. So they were more confident than ever in God's presence, and spoke the word with boldness. Do you not think theirs was a brave, happy life—full of love for God and enthusiasm for righteousness and confidence in the Divine protection.

What a grand lesson to learn. What matter anything if God be with us! Never mind what anybody says of us. (Inscription on walls of a Scotch college—"They say—What do they say?—Let them say!") Never mind what they try to do to us, if only we are certainly on the path of right. "Who is he that will harm you if ye be followers of that which is good?" "The Lord of hosts is with us. The God of Jacob is our Refuge!"

## LESSON XXI

# SPOILING CHRIST'S KINGDOM

*Acts IV. 32, to V. 17.*

### "An enemy hath done this."

Recapitulate last Lesson, briefly emphasizing the Courage and Confidence and Enthusiasm for God's service. What was the power that made them capable of this? Power of Holy Ghost at Pentecost. Now turn today from their public preaching and suffering and the persecutions of men, and see the effects of this power of the Holy Ghost on their ordinary life.

What two things are told of them in *v.* 32? Meaning of "one heart and one soul"? How many were they that were "of one heart and one soul"? (*v.* 4). Is this a usual thing to happen in this world? How did it happen? A great miracle, such miracles as Holy Ghost is performing always on men's souls. Here are 5,000 men of all varieties of age and character and position, of all varieties of opinion and temper and taste and feeling. Yet all in perfect agreement, because of their loving God and loving each other so thoroughly. That is what Holy Ghost always does, then and now.

Did their love consist merely in talking of love? How did they show it? They gave up all for each other's sake. Talk is cheap. Emotion is easy. But self-sacrifice is a thorough test. You remember our Lesson on St. Mark on Glory of Self-sacrifice? (Lesson VIII.) That was Christ's teaching to men, that self-sacrifice for God's sake and for others' sake was the grandest thing in the world. And now His disciples were learning His lesson. They cared only for God and their brethren. Cared not for self or money. Neither said any man that what he possessed was his own. They had one common fund; the rich put in all their riches, that the poor might share alike with themselves. They had learned Christ's lesson, that the true use of wealth was—what? Hoarding it up?—spending it all on our own fancies? No—doing good, serving God and their brethren.

Do you think their plan of community of goods was a very wise one? No. Even good men, filled with love and with power of Holy Ghost, can make mistakes. It would have been a beautiful plan if *all* were entirely perfect. But this wicked world spoiled its beauty. Poor workingmen had not to work to support their families—were supported free. Probably some got lazy; other people pretended to be Christians in order to get supported, and so on; and so after a while the Church sadly learned that the devil could spoil the beauty even of their lovely "Kingdom of God."

But if it were a mistake, was it not a glorious,

generous, noble mistake? Would you rather see a man make such mistake with a loving, generous motive, or see him letting the poor suffer through his selfish caution? Which would God rather see?

These early Christians were really trying to carry out our Lord's idea of founding a true "Kingdom of God" on earth. Remember our Lord's plan that He was so enthusiastic about. (St. Mark, Lesson II.) A "new earth, wherein dwelleth righteousness." A kingdom whose laws should be? The laws of Heaven. Whose glory should be? The glory of self-sacrifice. Whose power should be? Power of Love. Whose subjects should be of the character pictured in 1 Corinthians xiii. Tell me that character? Suffer long and are kind—envy not—seek not their own—bear all things—hope all things—endure all things."

Have we yet got very near to having this beautiful kingdom? No; but we are getting nearer to it. Where in Lord's prayer do we pray for it? This little period in the early Church was a grand attempt at it. But Satan spoiled it greatly. Could not bear to see such a lovely thing in the world. How did he spoil it? (1) By tempting the poor to laziness and hypocrisy. (2) By tempting the rich to pretend generosity.

Two specimens are picked out for us of the rich men. Who? Read iv. 36, 37; v. 1, 2. Be careful to notice that the historian is contrasting the two. The bad chapter division unfortunately spoils contrast. Contrast is between work of Holy Ghost in Barnabas and work of Satan in Ananias. What did Barnabas do? What sort of character was he? Ever hear of him again? What did Ananias do? Who shared his sin? Who tempted him? Why? In order to spoil Christ's lovely kingdom. Like a wicked boy spoiling another boy's beautiful things out of spite. Oh, what a shame, in the glory of that beautiful Christ life in the Church, to dash in that horrible thing of ugliness and sin! Ought it not make us angry with Satan? Make us hate him and resist him? Make us so ashamed when we join with him, like Ananias, and are disloyal to our Lord! But if it was Satan's fault why blame Ananias? Could he have helped doing what he did? See what Peter blames him for (*v.* 3). He is held responsible. He could have resisted. He made himself tool of Satan. He let Satan fill his heart. Who should have filled it? (ch. iv. 31). He let Satan come into the "temple of the Holy Ghost" (1 Corinthians vi. 19), and coax him to go against his Lord.

Now question fully on the whole story, ch. v. 1-17. (Notice proof that Holy Ghost is God in *vv.* 3, 4, "lied unto God.") Did Ananias really tell a lie? Did he speak at all? How could he then tell a lie? Yes. Acting a lie is just the same as saying it. Ananias said nothing. He simply walked in and laid down his money like Barnabas. But he tried to make the Church believe he was a generous, liberal Christian like Barnabas, full of love to God and man. Do boys and girls sometimes care more for good opinion of the Church than for that of God? Think more of comrades' good opinion than that of God's? Do they ever act a lie, and comfort themselves that they have not told one? Is there any difference in God's sight? Who condemned Ananias to death? Peter? Certainly not.

Probably Peter was as much surprised as anyone else. It was Christ who was watching so closely over every movement of the Church (see Lesson on Acts I.), and saw the need of a terrible punishment just then when men were joining with Satan to spoil his beautiful plan for the blessing and happiness of mankind. Apparently in Sapphira's case Peter knew that the same thing would happen as to her husband. But it was the Lord who struck them both dead. We have been thinking so much about His love that we are in danger of forgetting the sterner side. Sometimes sinners force Him to be stern; and, dearly though He loves poor sinners, He hates sin with an awful hatred. If terrible punishment is necessary to prevent terrible evil, He will inflict it.

See the effect—great fear. Yes, that effect sometimes necessary. Great shock to the Church—would have been greater shock, perhaps, if falsehood and hypocrisy seemed to be thriving unpunished. It taught men not to make light of God's holiness or presume too far on His loving patience. (See *v.* 13.) No more hypocrites or careless people dared to come into the Church of the holy Christ.

LESSONS.—

(1) Acted lie is same as spoken lie.

(2) Indignant resistance to Satan, the Lord's enemy, who is trying to make tools of us with which to spoil the Lord's blessed plans for good.

(3) What would make the Church to-day powerful and successful as in the first days? More of the power of the Holy Ghost, which we could have if in earnest

about it. We want to show the world this "one heart and one soul," instead of the wretched divisions of Christians who refuse to worship and work for God together. We want to show, also, that we believe Christ's theory of wealth, that the highest use of money is the service of God and our brethren. We want to show them, like the infant Church, the enthusiasm for God and Righteousness, the willingness to bear everything for Christ's sake—the beautiful lives, kindly, loving, unselfish, brightening and blessing all life around us. We should soon convert the "heathen at home" and the heathen abroad. We should soon force the world to believe in the "Kingdom of God" and in the power of the Holy Ghost.

## LESSON XXII

# FIGHTING AGAINST GOD

### Acts V. 17, VI. 18.

### "The rulers take counsel together against the Lord."

### § 1. The Secret of Strength

Title of Lesson to-day? Is it any use for people to "fight against God"? Who always wins in the end? Who fighting against God here? Why Sadducees? (See Lesson XX.) First thing done? (*v.* 18). Did it succeed? Why not? Could not keep these enthusiastic preachers quiet. Why? Filled with Holy Ghost, and therefore filled with love to their Master and enthusiasm for His work. Next thing tried? (*v.* 28). Was it any use? (*v.* 29). Think of the wonderful power and courage that comes from feeling oneself in the right! Here were, on the one hand, rulers and priests of high position, backed up by their bands of soldiers and police; and on the other hand a few unarmed, uneducated common men. Which conquered? Why? Obedience to God and Duty

132

and Righteousness is the great secret of power over others. If you are sure that you are in the right and have the approval of God, you have an inward feeling of courage and strength that enables you to dare all things. Not peculiar to Peter and Apostles. All brave, true men, living for God and Right, have such courage and strength.

## § 2. *Attitudes towards Religion*

Question closely on *vv*. 33-42. Interesting to remark that probably Paul was at this time one of Gamaliel's pupils (Acts xxii. 3). For the taxing (*v.* 37) refer to Luke ii. 1. Here are three different attitudes—(1) Enemies, (2) Neutrals, (3) Friends. Which in each class? So in the world to-day. (1) Men opposed to religion. Some wilfully, because they hate goodness. Many not wilfully—men brought up from childhood in unbelief, and with wrong thoughts of religion and of Christ. Will God blame both equally? (2) Neutrals—like Gamaliel. Cold, calculating men, not very enthusiastic for or against. He gives wise, cool advice to Sanhedrin. But he did not help religion much. Many like him. "Let it alone," they say; "don't bother about it, don't help it, and don't hinder it. If it succeed, let it succeed. If it fail, let it fail." And many add in their hearts what perhaps Gamaliel would not add—"We have something else to think of—our business and our newspapers and our amusements, etc. Let religion shift for itself without us." Is that a good attitude? (3) Friends—who are they? All who go to church and Sunday-school? No. What verse describes them? (*v.* 41). Those who are so determined on the side of the Kingdom of God that they will do or bear anything for Christ's sake, "rejoicing that they are counted worthy to suffer shame for His name." Our Lord tells who are his friends. "Ye are my friends if ye"? (John xv. 14).

## § 3. Evil Turned to Good

Read ch. vi. Remember last Lesson about community of goods. What did we think about the good of it? Was there any danger of evil? What? See it beginning here. Satan "fighting against God." It frequently happens that indiscriminate giving of alms breeds much mischief. Every clergyman in his parish knows of such. Idle people grumbling. "We don't get enough. Others get more. You are unfair. You are showing favouritism," etc. How saddening to the Apostles and the other noble, generous-hearted men and women who were giving up all for the sake of Christ and the brethren. But so it will be always in this poor, evil world. We should take courage that no new thing has happened unto us. Even in paradise Satan got admission. Even after Pentecost evil crept in.

The Apostles of course were at the head of all, and responsible for all. Think of them longing to keep their souls fitted for their highest work—Preaching, and Prayer, and Sacraments, and yet worried continually by this wretched grumbling about bread and money and clothing, and such like. What did they propose? (*v.* 3). Were they wise in this? Yes. Why? Is there such need in our day? Yes, very often. Sometimes the clergyman has not sufficient time for close thought and study to prepare good sermons because parish charities and building and all sorts of secular cares are put on him, which the lay people ought to look after. Think of that when you grow up.

But God wrought good out of the evil. How many orders of clergy are there in the church to-day? Yes. Bishops, priests, and deacons. So they were in the early Church. The Apostles were the bishops; the clergy ordained by them were the priests or presbyters. And here we have the deacons, originally, you see, appointed to "serve tables," look after poor, etc. So now, at ordination of a deacon, the bishop tells him that his duty is "to search for the sick, poor, and impotent people in the parish," etc. (See Ordination Service.) Who chose the deacons? But who ordained them? (*vv.* 5, 6). Yes. The choice lay with the people. But the ordaining them and sending them forth to minister lay with the Apostles, to whom the power was committed by our Lord. Ever since there have been these three orders of ministers in the Church. Our own old Church gives to the laity a great deal of power and choice in the selecting of their parish clergy and in the choosing even of their bishops. But the right of *commissioning* those chosen ones rests entirely with the bishops. They only have the power of making a deacon, ordaining a priest, or consecrating a bishop; so that the constitution of our Church today is as nearly as can be the same as that of the early Church.

### § 4. *Fighting against God*

Now, see the result of the "fighting against God" and against the spread of His Church (v. 41, 42; vi. 7). What an encouragement to think that God's eternal purposes cannot be defeated by men's opposition. Ever watched tide coming in? Could you stop it? Build a wall of sand to stop it—what happens? Soon it meets a rock and beats against it. Does this stop it? No; in a few minutes the rock is under water, and the tide sweeps on. Its waves rush in on the strand, but they seem to go back all the way every time. Do they? Sometimes three or four waves don't quite reach as far as the one before them. It seems as if tide were getting tired, going to give up defeated. Does it do so? No. In a moment more it sweeps on again with renewed power, *and never fails to fulfil its course.*

So with Church of Christ—the kingdom of God on earth. Think of its tide coming in through all the ages—has it had hindrances? Here is one in this chapter. Chapter after chapter we find them in this early history. Did they stop its progress? No. First, only 120 disciples. Then opposition. Then we find number in a few weeks 3,000. More opposition. Then number raised to 5,000. (Here again see vi. 7.) So through all the ages, hindrances—unbelief—false religions—persecutions—coldness and deadness of Christians—schisms and sects splitting up the Church, all seem to be checking the tide and delaying it. Are they? Yes. But can they finally put back the tide? No. Like the tide sweeping in from the ocean, so the great tide of God's purposes sweeps on till "the earth shall be full of the knowledge of the glory of the Lord, as the waters cover the sea."

## LESSON XXIII

# FAITHFUL UNTO DEATH

*Acts VI. 18; VII. 54 to VIII. 5.*

**"I will give thee a crown of life."**

Teacher should not attempt to deal with St. Stephen's speech except in the very brief summary of it in this Lesson. The chief object of the Lesson is to arouse admiration for a beautiful life lived for Christ, and desire to emulate such life in some degree at least.

Recapitulate. Why deacons appointed? Name them. What were their duties? Now, we have to talk about one especially. How described? (*v.* 8). A greater man probably than most of the Apostles. Why do you think not elected Apostle instead of Matthias? See ch. i. 21, 22. He could not be a "witness of Resurrection" as he probably had not seen the Lord. Yet, though so clever and holy and great, he took lowest place—going to see the widows and poor, and seek and look after their food and comforts, doing common, lowly things well for Christ's sake. But, being "filled with the Holy Ghost," he could not but show it. Could you carry about dried rose leaves concealed? Perfume would be discovered. So with real religion of man filled with Holy Ghost. Nonsense to think as some people do, "I have real religion, but I never show it." It may be that you don't *talk about it*, which for children may be a good thing; but if you have it, it cannot be hid. Your life *must* show it. If not, it is because you have not got it.

Stephen's enthusiastic religion could not be hid. Gradually the widows and the sick and the poor began to talk much about him, his holiness, wisdom, miracles. Then outsiders began to take notice—to listen to his teaching—to watch his beautiful life. Then jealousy and hostility began, perhaps because of the crowds of disciples and great company of the priests coming to Christ (*v.* 7). Congregations of foreign Jews in Jerusalem (name them, *v.* 9) began to dispute with him. Notice "them of Cilicia." Tarsus was in Cilicia, and Saul of Tarsus was in Jerusalem then. Think of these two young men meeting in debate. Saul very clever. In intellect quite a match for Stephen or for any man. But he and his comrades could not resist (*v.* 10). Why? Because Stephen had on his side truth, and the "wisdom and spirit of God."

Not pleasant to be defeated in open argument. Very irritating. What did they do? (*v.* 11). I don't believe Saul had a share in that. He was too high a type of man for that, even before his conversion. What did they say? (*v.* 11). Do you think it was true? Probably some truth in it. The worst lie to defend oneself against is the "half truth."

"You may face a lie outright,
But a lie that is half the truth is
a harder matter to fight."

Show me that this was exactly what happened in our Lord's case also? (Mark xiv. 5-8). Stephen had a broader mind and a wider view of truth than any of the Apostles then. He was the forerunner of St. Paul's broad views. He could see that Christianity was not to be a mere branch of Judaism, that Judaism must vanish away. Probably said something like what our Lord said (John iv. 21; Mark xiii. 2). Such words could be easily twisted just then when the people were in a frenzy of jealousy for Mosaic institutions. So nowadays if a man is decidedly Low Church or Broad Church or High Church, his words are often twisted to look like dissent or unbelief or Romanism. Very wicked and dishonest to do such things.

See the clever malice. This was just the cry to stir up "the people," who had been friendly before (*v.* 12). So poor Stephen had not only the rulers and Pharisees against him, but also the howling, raging mob. What did they do and say? (*vv.* 12-14). Did he care? Not he! Truth at any cost! Do you think God does not rejoice in fearlessness like that for truth's sake?

The King of France told Palissy the potter, "If you don't give up your Protestant opinions, I shall be compelled to give you up to the Inquisition." To which the brave potter replied, "You are a king, yet you say you will be *compelled;* I am only a potter, but no one can *compel* me to do wrong; I can die for the right, but I cannot give it up." This is the spirit that God loves.

"He's a slave who dares not choose
Hatred, scoffing, and abuse,
Rather than in silence shrink
From the truth he needs must think.
He's a slave who dares not be
In the right with two or three."

Picture the trial—the hostile people crowding around the judges on the high bench, Annas and Caiaphas and Gamaliel probably amongst them. The men of Cilicia and Cyrene amongst the accusers. One young man especially, who never forgot this trial, to whose recollection probably we owe the story. Who? And the prisoner brave and calm and quiet in the midst of it all. He listens to the lying charge. The natural feeling would be indignation at the lie, and perplexity as he saw it had some truth and would be hard to deny, and fear at the attitude of the judges and people. Were those Stephen's feelings? Calm and serene he looked at the excited crowd, and all saw his face as if —what? (*v.* 15). With God's friendship and approval, why should he care for men's anger! Angel faces come from angel characters. Do you believe that a life of wickedness affects appearances of a face? *e.g.,* drunkenness, ill-temper, etc. If we let evil possess us, it will write its mark on our faces. So goodness, nobleness, holiness. Sometimes a very plain man or woman looks quite beautiful owing to a good and noble expression of face. I read once of a saintly missionary called by the Indians "Gloryface." God sends us into the world with a face on which to write good or evil record. Let us mark a lovely record on it by a lovely life.

Now listen to Stephen's speech. Not a word of self-defence—or fear—or effort to escape. He quietly leaves all that in God's hand, and uses his opportunity of straight and fearless speaking to them. "Have I said that God's majestic presence not confined to temples made with hands? Well, did not Isaiah say the same? Have I denounced the vanity of sacrifices and offerings unworthily offered? Your prophets have done the same. I have spoken the truth, and by it I stand." And then, as he sees the anger and fierce opposition rising in their faces, he lets fearlessly forth his righteous indignation. He could bear lies against himself, but not resistance against God. What does he say? "Ye stiffnecked and uncircumcised," etc. (*vv.* 51-53). Yes, their repeated defiance of God rouses his holy indignation. Was his anger wrong? Is anger ever right? (Ephesians iv. 26). Was our Lord ever angry? (Mark iii. 5). Moral indignation is a necessity to keep the world sweet and pure. In wilful sin there must be no flattery or compliments, but determined, straight speaking, whether it offend or not.

What a rage they were in! Describe it? (*vv.* 54-57). Poor Stephen! his martyrdom was very close now. Where did he look for sympathy and help? To judges? to the Roman police? No (*v.* 55). Looked up steadfastly *into heaven.* What did he see? Jesus *standing* as in attitude of help. What a glorious comfort to him at the hour of death! Often God grants such sights to dying people. Often they cry out to Him with glowing eyes and hands stretched forth eagerly as if seeing heaven. Did the people believe Stephen? Yet one amongst them within two years saw the same sight, and was converted by it. Who? (Acts ix.)

Now comes the end. Rough mob law. He is dragged through the streets to the rock of stoning, and flung down about twelve feet. (Lightfoot: *Horæ Hebraicæ.*) Then the witnesses prepare to throw great stones on him, and lay by their robes. Who holds them? How he must have wondered at the fearless young deacon. Could he ever, all his life, forget that noble prayer, as the poor crushed youth lifts up his hands to the open heaven and the watching Christ? What was the prayer? For safety? For vengeance? What? (*v.* 60). Like what other prayer? (Luke xxii. 34). St. Augustine says that that prayer won St. Paul for the Church (*Si Stephenus non orasset, ecclesia Paulum non haberet,* "If Stephen had not prayed, the Church would not have had Paul.")

How is his death described? (*v.* 60). When we want to go to sleep we like quietness and closed shutters. Poor Stephen had to go to sleep in the midst of agony and noise. Is it not a beautiful description of a Christian's death, like a tired child going to sleep in the dark night to waken in the glorious sunshine? The early Christians loved this thought. Epitaphs on Catacombs—"Victoria sleeps;" "Zokeus is here laid to sleep;" "Arethusa sleeps in God;" "Clementia, tortured, dead, sleeps, will rise again."

Lessons. —

(1) Could you be a martyr for Christ? Not necessarily to bear death, but to bear loss, or mockery, or dislike of comrades? Do you care enough for Christ to do and

bear unpleasant things for His sake? It may be the only martyrdom asked of you. Very little compared with Stephen's. But if the Lord expected even that much of you, would He be disappointed?

(2) See close of last Lesson about "tide flowing in." Here is another assault—resistance to progress of the Church. Did it stop it? No. See persecution arose (ch. viii. 1), which scattered them all abroad, and therefore spread the Gospel more than ever. See Stephen replaced by Paul, the greatest of all the Apostles. "The blood of the martyrs is the seed of the Church."

# GOOD TIDINGS OF GREAT JOY

*Acts VIII. 5 to end.*

**"The fruit of the Spirit is . . . joy."**

About whom was last Lesson? What was he? Name another famous deacon? This chapter almost entirely about Philip. When Stephen was struck down Philip took his place. What great trouble came on the Church after Stephen's death? Persecutors led by whom? (*v.* 3). How did God bring good out of this trouble? (*v.* 5). What lesson for us? Probably the Christians thought it was hard on them, and wondered that God should allow it—perhaps some began to doubt Christ's constant care. Not till long afterwards could they see God's good purpose—the spreading of the Gospel. So with many of our troubles. We see no reason for them. We doubt and grumble and perhaps only in the Kingdom above shall we ever understand the good purpose of God in them.

## § 1. *Baptizing into the Kingdom*

Now, tell me the whole story of Philip and Simon Magus? (Question briskly on *vv.* 6-24.) Prepare questions carefully to bring out the important points. Remember O. T. case like Simon? Another in N. T.? (Exodus vii. 11, etc.; Acts xix. 13-19). Do you think Simon's were real miracles? What great difference in Philip's which made the people believe? (1) Very simple—no ranting or incantations or magical rites. (2) Unselfish, not for gaining money or "giving out that himself was some great one." (3) The whole teaching that accompanied his miracles appealed to the best instincts of the people. He *preached Christ* unto them (*v.* 5). Christ's love, holiness, unselfishness, service of man, Christ's Death and Resurrection to give hope to the world. He preached Christ's dearest project for the world, "the Kingdom of God" (*v.* 12)—the kingdom on earth, whose laws were to be the laws of Heaven, whose subjects were to be pure and noble and unselfish—in some degree like the self-sacrificing Christ Himself. That was the ideal of the Church on earth. Man that was made in the image of God seldom falls so low that he cannot admire such a kingdom. Many of these Samaritans entered that kingdom. How? (*v.* 12). Have you entered it? How? Take care to be faithful in it. Did Philip say it did not matter about Baptism if they only believed? (*vv.* 12-38). Who commanded Baptism? Therefore, must never think lightly of it—never neglect it. What was the result of founding the "Kingdom of God" on Samaria? (*v.* 8). "Much joy" for the glad tidings and the blessed, helpful miracles. That is always result of real religion. Remember this, as we have to refer again to it at close.

### § 2. *Confirmation*

Now see Collect in Confirmation Service. The bishop says: "We make our humble supplications unto Thee for these Thy servants, upon whom, after the example of Thy holy Apostles, we have now laid our hands." Where do we find this "example"? See *vv.* 14-18. See also ch. xix. 5, 6. The deacons and the lay Christians preached and baptized, but to the Apostles the higher powers belonged. Perhaps this was necessary to keep the Church from splitting up into separate bodies of Christians, owning no allegiance to the Apostles, and not connected with the mother Church in any way. The Church has kept up the custom: the bishop is still a centre of unity—no clergyman can be ordained, no child confirmed without him. This central authority helps to prevent divisions. Is Confirmation in our day only a mere form? Certainly not. We believe that through the power of God in the Church the grace of the Holy Ghost is conferred in Confirmation by the imposition of the bishop's hands. Therefore we speak of a child going not merely "to confirm" his promises and vows, but *to be confirmed, i.e., strengthened,* by the power of the Holy Ghost for the struggles of the Christian life. Confirmation is to us the completing of Holy Baptism. Therefore look forward solemnly and hopefully to it by-and-by.

(In senior classes it may be pointed out that St. Peter

(*v.* 14) was *not the sender*, but *sent* by the Apostles. No
trace in the history of the early Church of the theory of
Supremacy of Peter. The supreme rule belonged to no
one man, but to the entire apostolate. So to-day the rule
of the Church belongs to the entire episcopate, not to
any individual bishop, whether in Rome or Canterbury
or Armagh.)

## § 3. The Joy of Religion

Eastern picture. A hot road, white in the blinding
sunlight—lonely—silent—deserted. Now a cloud of
dust, a trampling of camels and horses, and a splendid
chariot with its guards and outriders dashing along, and
in it a black negro man, gorgeously dressed, earnestly
reading a parchment roll. Who and what was he?
Where had he been? What for? Therefore a Jew either
by conversion or by descent. Black Jews found long
afterwards. (There is now in Cambridge a strange old
red goatskin roll of part of Hebrew Bible that has been
found in the synagogue of the Black Jews of Malabar in
1806.) See the puzzled look of the black reader. What is
he reading? Whom does it refer to? What puzzles him?
Probably had heard in Jerusalem of Stephen's death and
excitement about Christ. Just in a fit state for learning
about Christ. And just then suddenly, "by chance" as
it seems to him, his carriage overtakes a solitary man,
who startles him with a strange question. What? Tell
me their conversation.

What a great deal depended on that "chance"
meeting, both for the eunuch and probably for his

nation. Probably first message of the Gospel to Africa. Was it really chance? Why not? (*v.* 26). So with many of our "chance" meetings and events. Often a man's whole future is altered through his chance coming home by one road rather than another, meeting and talking "by chance" to some man—reading "by chance" some book, hearing "by chance" some sermon. (Give instances, if possible.) Sometimes, looking back on such "chances" afterwards, one feels solemnly that many chance things must be as much guided by God as was Philip's meeting with the eunuch. At any rate, all "chances" will be blessed to him whose life is being lived under the guidance of God.

Something else to be learned. Here is an untaught man puzzling over the Scriptures—like Luther when he found Bible in monastery at Erfurt—not content to throw them aside when difficult to understand. He was *very* eager to know about God. Not many people *very* eager. A great many care a *little* about religion —enough to make them go to church, and keep from grave evil. But the man that really wins the happiness and blessing of religion is the man who is true to the little light he has, who says, "If there be a God, I am *determined* to find Him—if His blessing be possible to win, I am *determined* to win it." Of such was this eunuch. God always helps such. Like Cornelius. (ch. x.) The path of duty is the path towards finding Christ. The desire to learn and willingness to be taught are the great preparations for conversion. Therefore this Ethiopian *at once* decides for Christ. It may endanger his high position. No matter. "What doth hinder me," etc. (*v.* 37).

Evidently Baptism formed part of Philip's teaching to him, as of Peter (ch. ii. 38).

So he went on his way *rejoicing*, and we see him no more. But we in thought follow him with interest to his own land. Tradition says he converted Queen Candace and many of her people—perhaps he prepared the way for the later period when the nation became Christian, and the prophecy was fulfilled—"Ethiopia shall stretch," etc. (Psalms lxviii. 31). But all we know with certainty is that he went on *rejoicing*.

So does every boy and girl and man and woman who is really living for our Lord. That would be the cure for gloom and fret everywhere. (See *v.* 8.) "Much joy in that city." Why? Look at cities to-day, with their crowds, their poor, their grasping struggle and worry of life. How make them glad? Try Philip's plan. Want to teach you, children, that the secret of purest, highest joy is true membership in the "Kingdom of God." Young people often think religion gloomy. Why? Perhaps because older Christians have gloomy faces, and find fault with fun and games and amusements. Never be misled by these gloomy, mistaken people, who have not enough of knowledge of Christ's character to make them rejoice in religion. To be members of Christ's Kingdom will but increase all your pleasures and purify all your life. "Much joy is always the result of true religion, of beautiful lives. Does God like to see you, boys and girls, at games and pleasures, romping and rejoicing like the lambs in the field. What only does He forbid you? Yes. Sin, which would spoil your lives. He longs to see beautiful souls and beautiful deeds, and He wants to see you very happy. See Lesson VI. on St. Mark.

# LESSON XXV

# EASTER

*EPISTLE—Colossians III. 1, etc.*

*GOSPEL—St. John XX. 1, etc.*

Our Prayer Book has two Epistles and Gospels for Easter Day. The Easter story told in both Gospels is almost the same, and it has been already dealt with in the Lesson on St. Mark xvi.—"The Resurrection." Let the teacher read that Lesson carefully for teaching the story, and then go on with the further Easter Lessons as taught below.

Name of day? Meaning? Commemorate what? (Now question on Resurrection story as indicated in Lesson, Mark xvi.) Did disciples expect Resurrection? How do you know? Why not expect it? Too wonderful to believe. Why did they believe it at last? Because they saw it, and were thoroughly convinced of it. Why do you believe that I am teaching this class to-day? Have you any doubt about it? Apostles felt like that. Mary saw Him—and Peter—and the men at Emmaus, and the eleven disciples, and Thomas—and the 500 brethren, etc. Were they glad? Why?

Have *we* any reason to be glad about it? Would it matter to us if story not true, if disciples really stole away body while soldiers slept? Why should it matter to us?

### § 1. Makes us sure that Jesus was God.

Resurrection most important proof of this. One had come on earth not to be distinguished in appearance from other men. But He said that He was God. That He had come down to die for men—that through His death there was forgiveness of sins—that if a man believed in Him, though he were dead, yet should he live, etc. And people said, "This would be blessed news if true, but it is not." "Aye, but it is true," said the Apostles, and "God has proved it in that He raised Him from the dead.

This the Apostles especially insisted on. They pledged the very existence of Christianity to the truth of it. "If Christ be not risen, then is our preaching vain, and your faith is also vain." See 1 Corinthians xv. 12-19. In the Acts of the Apostles we find it was the main subject of their preaching, and the main thought about themselves was as "witnesses of the Resurrection." See Acts i. 8, 21, 22; iii. 15; iv. 2, 33; xvii. 18; xxiv. 21, etc. "We are sure of it," they said. "We are witnesses. We twelve men saw Jesus of Nazareth. Some of us lived near Him as boys. We lived with Him as men. We saw Him work miracles; saw Him arrested, tried, crucified, dead. And then we saw Him risen again—and if you don't believe us, ask the 500 brethren and the others who saw Him. We are sure, positively and certainly.

Therefore we know that Christ is God, and that we may depend on all that He told us of His power and glory, and the heaven by-and-by."

And because they were so sure they could bear everything—trouble, torture, imprisonment. "We don't care," they said, "the Lord Jesus is risen—gone up to heaven. He sees it all. We are only glad to bear anything or do anything for Him."

### § 2. Makes us sure that we shall rise again.

What an enormous difference that would make in this poor world of sorrow and death! Think of the world before Christ—and poor heathen world to-day. Think of poor mother breaking her heart over her dead child. Tell you of funeral 2,000 years ago. A girl, daughter of a great wise Roman named Cicero—beautiful procession—people standing silent around—mother sobbing—father pale and stern, but too proud to cry over his dead child. No one to comfort him but one old friend named Sulpicius, who had written him a letter of comfort. Poor old man, it was the best comfort that he could give. Should you like to hear it? "Don't fret," he said; "everybody must die—it is only a girl—remember that you are the great wise Cicero. You should, therefore, have great fortitude. You should be too proud to cry over your dead child." That was all the comfort he could give. What a miserable comfort! Then came the priests in their stately robes to sing the sad burial words at the tomb. Guess what they sang? "There will be no parting there"? "Safe in the arms of Jesus"? Ah! no. This is their hymn: "Vale, vale, in aeternum vale," i.e., "Farewell, farewell, for ever and ever, farewell!" Alas for the poor sorrowing pagan world who did not know of Christ and Easter. What a glad thing for us who do! How we should rejoice and thank God! How we should pray for His grace that some of us might be sent out by-and-by to the poor heathen, to comfort their poor sorrowful hearts with the Easter story.

What should we be able to tell the poor heathen mother about Easter to make her heart glad? (1) That we know Jesus Christ was God, He who took the children in His arms; and therefore we know God's feelings towards the children. (2) That He promised that there should be an eternal life after death, and proved it by rising Himself after death. (3) That, therefore a poor mother can with fearless heart commit her dying child to Him who loved the little children. Death is now for us but the threshold of the great glad eternal life. The dying child is but as the dying caterpillar on the leaf, who shall by-and-by burst its withered shell and soar out in the sunshine a glorious butterfly. "Them also that sleep in Jesus will God bring with Him; wherefore comfort one another with these words." (1 Thessalonians iv. 14, 18).

If there is time, emphasize here the lesson of the Epistle for the day—"Seek the things which are above," for "when Christ, who is our life, shall appear, then shall ye also appear with Him in glory." Therefore let us live as those with such noble prospects before us ; and let us go forth to-day with bounding hearts, thanking God for this glad Easter Gospel. Let all around us this springtime remind us of the Easter message when the world of nature is arising from its winter death, and every budding hedge and every leafy tree is like a message of God to earth preaching "Jesus and the Resurrection."

# LESSON XXVI

# ASCENSION DAY

*EPISTLE—Acts I. 1.*

*GOSPEL—St. Mark XVI. 14.*

Read Epistle and Gospel, and also Luke xxiv. 50, etc. Out of all combined teach the Ascension story. Read the Lesson Acts i. Aim at exciting awe, wonder, reverence. Children now-a-days are in danger of being too free and familiar with our Lord's name, and not sufficiently reverent or impressed with His greatness and glory.

Try to influence this generation of Church children with the importance of keeping Ascension Day. See in Communion office how the Church has placed it on a par with the four great Festivals, giving it a "Proper Preface" for itself. We need a great improvement in this matter. The result of this neglect is a growing haziness and almost doubt about this great fact of the Ascension.

In the past six weeks the Church has commemorated two of the most important events in the life of our Lord— Calvary and the Resurrection. After the Resurrection something else must happen. The Ascension. Why?

Because if the Lord did not go back into heaven, then He must be here in bodily presence still, which He is not, or He must have grown old and weak and died again, like any ordinary man, which would be a very poor ending for His wonderful life. Therefore we are quite prepared to hear of Ascension. We should be quite puzzled at the whole story of Christ if no Ascension.

Now see the story in Epistle and Gospel for day. Read also Luke xxiv. 50. St. Luke had, perhaps, learned more about Ascension when he wrote Acts. Picture scene. A little band of twelve men moving through suburbs of Jerusalem to the Bethany road over the lower slopes of Mount of Olives. Ever been on that road before? Tell me of any occasions? Yes. Very tender associations. He had often walked wearily there, looking forward to friendly greetings in somebody's house at Bethany. Whose? There the disciples had gone with Him when Lazarus raised. They would remember that now. But more solemn and sad memories. They cross over Kedron again. When before? They walk near Gethsemane, where He had struggled in His awful agony, and where they all forsook Him and fled. What a strange walk, never to be forgotten, would be this last walk with the Lord! What a remembrance in after days that scene on the mountain top! There He stood in His mysterious Resurrection body, listening patiently to their questions about the times and the seasons, and directing them about their great missionary work "to the uttermost part of the earth." There the most wonderful thing in the world's history about to take place. Did the world take any notice? No. Not even Jerusalem, which lay so near. Herod and Pontius Pilate and the priests and the busy merchants were all about their own work, and took no notice. Angels would be watching eagerly for the return of the Lord to heaven, but the world then, as now, did not trouble much about Him.

Ah! the world had not been kind to Him! He had lived a life that seemed so certain to win love; but they would not love Him, they preferred a murderer to Him. Even the little group who stood round Him now to say good-bye—had they been kind to Him? Peter who denied—Thomas who doubted—the rest who forsook Him. But did He remember and remind them of their faults just now? Ah, no! The cross and the desertion and the ingratitude had not embittered Him in the least. In loving, tender farewell He lifted up His hands and blessed them. And while He blessed them what happened? (Luke xxiv. 51). Is it not a pleasant thought, the last sight men ever saw of Christ was while His lips were uttering words of love and His hands were stretched out in blessing? Did you ever go to see off at boat or train some relative or close friend? Would you not remember how they looked when saying good-bye? Always think about the last view of the Lord saying good-bye. It was "just like Him," as we say. Just like all His life of kindness and love.

Did they see Him go up into heaven? What hindered? (Acts i. 9). They could not see up. Could He still see down? Do you think He was still blessing? So to-day that cloud between us. Can we see Him? Can He see us? Do you think He cares what we are doing? Do you think He is blessing us still?

How startled the Apostles were—staring up wonderingly, longingly. Perhaps they wanted to go too, or wanted Him to come back to them. Who spoke to them? Perhaps the two angels that had been in tomb. Perhaps "two men," Moses and Elias, who in shining apparel had come to Him before. When? (Mark ix. 4). What did they say? Was it wrong to be looking—longing after Christ? No ; better if we looked and longed more. Why blame them? Because Christ had left them plenty of work to do for Him, and they were to go and busy themselves about it (*v.* 8), and not be merely sentimentalizing. What was the promise they gave? When shall He so come? Second Advent. In *like* manner—what manner? Blessing His people. He went away to heaven blessing His disciples, and He will come back blessing them. And meantime? Still blessing. Do we look forward to this coming? Gentleman left his boy in a great crush at East India House, promising to come back for him. In the hurry of business he forgot him until evening. Rushed back in great fright. Boy standing wearily where he had left him. "I knew you would come back, father; you said you would."

Will His coming be a joy and blessing to everybody? Why not? What an awful thing if we missed His blessing. "We believe that Thou shalt come to be our Judge; we therefore pray Thee," etc. (Te Deum).

Now think what the Ascension has gained for us. Here is the great Victor, the fierce conflict over, going to receive His crown. Ancient victors in their processions scattered gifts among the crowd. So the Lord, victorious now. How pleasant to Him to think of how He had borne the Temptation, the Agony, the Cross, all for men. So shall we feel whenever we have conquered temptation for His sake. Now the resistless Victor returning to be crowned. "Highly exalted, and given a name above every name." "Captain of our salvation." "Head over all things to His Church." Scattering His glorious gifts. (Read Psalms lxviii. 18.) Ascended on high, received gifts for men; yea, even for the rebellious." What gifts? (1) The gift of salvation for every poor sinner who comes unto God through Him. (2) The gift of Immortality, and the assurance of it through seeing Him rise from the dead and ascend into heaven. (3) The gift of His eternal Presence. Seems a strange thing to say when He was going away. Yet true. His presence no longer confined to one place at one time, He was again to be Omnipresent, pervading all creation. Illustrate—lamp on ground in a crowd only gives light to a few. When lifted up high it shines on all. (4) The gift of the Holy Ghost. (See Acts ii. 33.) "He hath shed forth this." For some mysterious reason while He was here in bodily form the Holy Ghost could not come. "But if I depart, I will send Him unto you." See the startling difference. The first sermon after Pentecost made more converts than the Lord's whole life on earth. A marvellous electrical power was over all. Who sent Holy Ghost, the Comforter, to put life into the Church, to rouse good thoughts, to help us towards God?

> "Whose gentle voice we hear,
> Soft as the breath of even;
> That checks each fault, that calms each fear.
> And speaks of heaven."

What great festival celebrates the coming of Holy Ghost? When will it be? We have been trying to sympathize with our Lord in His sufferings for us, in the glory of His self-sacrifice. Now let us sympathize with Him in His victory and His joy. Let us lift up our hearts to Him gratefully to the heaven where He is gone, and pray that we may in heart and mind thither ascend, and with Him continually dwell (Collect for Ascension Day).

# WHITSUNDAY

*EPISTLE—Acts II. 1-12.*

*GOSPEL—St. John XIV. 15-31.*

Read carefully Lesson II. on Acts of Apostles. Try to impress on yourself and the children the grand power within reach of all. Half the weakness and poorness of Christian life is because men do not "believe in the Holy Ghost."

What commemorate to-day? What is this day called? Why so called? You would easily understand if you lived in the early days, 1500 years ago, when Whitsunday was especially the "White Sunday?" It was one of the great baptismal seasons of the year, in memory of that day on which the Apostles had been baptised with the Holy Ghost. Christians met together on the "White Sunday" to receive into the congregation of Christ's Church those who had been admitted by Holy Baptism. In robes of pure white they entered the church, in token of the purity of life which Baptism denoted, while the chants of praise rose from the congregations for the white-robed throngs of spiritual children who in Baptism had been "born of water and the Spirit."

From very earliest times, even, it is said, from the days of the Apostles, the Church has kept this festival of Whitsuntide to commemorate—what? Yes, the most important event, perhaps, in the whole history of the world. Want you to understand to-day how important, and *what an enormous difference the fact of Pentecost made.*

### § 1. The Gospel

First turn to Gospel of the day. What does our Lord say in promising that Holy Ghost should come? How long should He stay with them? Should He be visible in human form like our Saviour? (*v.* 17). Shall be *in you."* What should He do for them? (*v.* 26). Did anybody else in N. T. prophesy of Holy Ghost? (Matthew iii. 11). Did anybody in O. T.? Many. See especially in chapter from which Epistle is taken. Who? What had he prophesied? (Acts ii. 16-18). Did our Lord repeat promise of Holy Ghost after Resurrection? (Acts i. 8). What specially promised there as result of His coming? Yes. Power was the great need of these few weak, simple, ignorant Christians who were to conquer the world for Christ. Power was the great need of all the converts who were to be members of Christ's "Kingdom of God." (See Lesson I on Acts of Apostles) What had they to promise? Same as we who are now by Baptism made members of that "Kingdom of God." What? Third answer in Catechism. Is it easy to renounce devil—to keep God's holy will and commandments? Which is easier, to be bad or good? Only by some miraculous power can we succeed. And this miraculous power was the gift of Pentecost. We shall learn more about this power later on in Lesson.

## § 2. *The Epistle*

We have talked of promise that Holy Ghost should come. Now turn to Epistle, and see what happened when He did come. *(For this Lesson on the Epistle see Lesson II on Acts of the Apostles.)*

## § 3. *The Power of the Holy Ghost*

Now let us try to understand about the Holy Ghost. Just remember that this is God. Can we see Him? Feel Him? How? By His promptings within He speaks through conscience. Makes you feel His blame or praise. If you struck your mother, how should you feel? If you gave up something very pleasant to you for the sake of a sick comrade, how should you feel? That is the Holy Spirit's way of blaming and approving. Think how solemn! God really within us, rejoicing at every good deed, pained at every bad one. Do people all feel this blame and approval? Yes, cannot help it. Do all obey? No. Then He is pained. Why does He want us to do the right and good always? Because He loves us, wishes us well, grieves to see us do what makes us bad and wretched. How good of God to care so much for us. (See Ephesians iv. 30.) Now you know meaning of grieving Him.

But is it enough merely to urge us to do right? No. We cannot do it. We often try and fail, and only sometimes succeed. But God dwelling within us does more. What? (Acts i. 8). POWER. What sort of power? Power to be good, holy, full of enthusiastic self-sacrifice for God and for righteousness. Most important to believe in this *power*. This is what makes that Pentecost Day so important. A new power came into life—to be the gift of every disciple of Christ for ever, if he would but reach out for it and use it. No one now *need be conquered* by evil. Great loss that people don't believe more in Holy Ghost. Illustrate—a man in sure danger from robbers, and an army within hearing who would help him if he called out, or a weak man whose whole happiness depends on accomplishing a task too great for him, and help is near, but he does not know—does not believe it. What is the great distinction between Christianity and all other forms of religion? THIS POWER. Other teachers could tell men to try to do right. Christ gives men *power to do it*.

Even in Old Testament days the Church of God had not that power. A few men here and there got it by special inspiration; but it was not within the reach of all men, as now. They had cravings for good and efforts after right; but, compared with the great power of the Holy Ghost that Christ has given, their illumination and power was but—

"Like as moonlight unto sunlight, and as water unto wine."

See the power that came to these early Christians—the courage and self-sacrifice and enthusiasm about religion. In 100 years they had spread religion through the Roman Empire. Look at this sermon of St. Peter's, bearding priest and Pharisee and mob in Jerusalem itself, charging them with killing God's Anointed. (v. 23). Peter, who a few weeks before was afraid of a maid-servant. See the effect of that great sermon of the Christian Church. (*vv.* 37-41). Why? Power of Holy Ghost. Look at what St. Paul, who received the gift long afterwards, says of its effect on his own life and that of others. (Galatians v. 22). See what a power it is in the lives of the holiest, noblest people you know. (Emphasize this to make the Holy Ghost appear a real power whose effects they can see.)

LESSONS.—

(1) *Believe in the Holy Ghost.* Recognise His promptings in you all day long. In your Baptism that power began, and will be with you all your life unless you wilfully drive it away. (See Baptismal Service.) Be very sure that that power is there, that you need not be beaten in the fight with sin unless you choose.

(2) *Grieve not the spirit.*—(Ephesians iv. 30). How could you? (a) by resisting His promptings; (b) by not using or caring for His help. He is the best friend you ever had. His great longing and craving is to make you holy and happy. (Romans viii. 26). Yet so many disappoint Him. Think of a farmer looking at a field where he had sown good seed and taken exceeding great

pains, and seeing poor stunted growth, he turns away in sorrow: "Well, that field has disappointed me sadly!"

(3) *Quench not the Spirit.*—Some even go so far as to quench His influence altogether. (1 Thessalonians v. 19). What an awful possibility! To push away the only hand that can lead us to Christ and to heaven. Yet it is possible. Pray—"O God the Holy Ghost, proceeding from the Father and the Son, have mercy upon us, miserable sinners!"